The Last ILLUSION

I0459644

The Last
ILLUSION

Izek Aliev

Copyright © 2022 by Izek Aliev

All rights reserved. No part of this publication may be reproduced, distributed, or transmitted in any form or by any means, including, photocopying,recording, or other electronic or mechanical methods, without the prior written permission of the copyright owner and the publisher, except in the case of brief quotations embodied in critical reviews and certain other noncommercial uses permitted by copyright law. For permission requests, write to the publisher, addressed "Attention: Permissions Coordinator," at the address below.

ARPress
45 Dan Road Suite 5
Canton MA 02021

Hotline: 1(888) 821-0229
Fax: 1(508) 545-7580

Ordering Information:
Quantity sales. Special discounts are available on quantity purchases by corporations, associations, and others. For details, contact the publisher at the address above.

Printed in the United States of America.
ISBN-13:   Paperback   979-8-89330-912-6
              eBook   979-8-89330-911-9

Library of Congress Control Number: 2024902573

CONTENTS

In the beginning was the Word,
and the Word was with God,
and the Word was God.

PROLOGUE

The second millennium was coming to an end. Most people had a sense of excitement and expectation for something new. After all, the change of the millennium was a serious event, even for the most ardent atheists. On the eve of the millennium, some people were afraid of man-made disasters, others of natural cataclysms, and some of them longed for some kind of miracle, even in the form of the end of the world. However, all these people were united by the feeling of their own chosenness, the awareness that it was they who were destined to open a page of the third millennium since the birth of Christ.

Chapter 1

On September 22, 1999, the weather in New York City was perfectly summery. It was quite warm on the first day of fall (1). Everyone was wearing shorts and T-shirts.

For several years now the weather has been autumnal in this city until almost mid-January. The seasons sort of shifted in time. Late winter came around February, and the cold air didn't recede almost until April. Snow fell and lay for only a few days, but it inevitably paralyzed the whole metropolis. News programs were choked with panic, which was immediately relayed to citizens. Schools were closed, transportation was irregular and barely functional. Huge snowplows cleared the streets intensively, but, strangely enough, the opposite effect was achieved: the dirt only smeared on the asphalt and spread throughout the neighborhood. Young fellows with shovels scurried around in the hope of earning money, helping the owners of cars to dig their vehicles out of the two-day snowdrift.

This chaos lasted no more than three days and then the sun appeared from behind the clouds, and the streets were naturally cleared. At that moment, it seemed to people that the three nightmare days were as if they had never happened.

The silver Bentley was speeding down the Belt Parkway toward the country's main airport, JFK, as Americans call it in honor of one of their most beloved presidents, John Fitzgerald Kennedy.

The highway winds along the shoreline of a huge bay, bounding the colossal massif of New York City to the southeast, which many residents of the world rightly consider the capital of the world. The city stretches in a narrow corridor along the mouth of the Hudson River, which turns into a naturally sheltered harbor formed by a wide channel and a lot of islands, the largest of which are Manhattan, Staten Island, and Long Island. On either side of the high-speed road stretched green swaths of densely planted man-made forest.

(1 The day of the autumnal equinox, considered the astronomical boundary between summer and fall.)

As the luxury car majestically sliced through the air, it seemed to leave behind the simpler cars that were ashamed and gave way to it. A young man with soft, curly light-brown hair was behind the wheel. His high forehead, sunken cheeks, elongated, slightly hooked nose, and thin lips made his face look noble. He could have looked like Jesus Christ himself if he had added a mustache, a beard, and long hair to his portrait. Of course, this was not typical for a man of Jewish descent. Although the same could be said of the Son of God.

Joseph (that was the man's name) was visibly nervous and glanced from time to time at the clock built into the mahogany panel. For reassurance, he kept checking it against the Rolex on his left hand, the dial of which was studded with tiny diamonds that gleamed dazzlingly in the sunlight. Both showed the same time - 3:28 PM. It was thirty-two minutes before the registration ended, and the young man pressed harder on the gas pedal.

Joseph loved his Rolex. It was a gift from the company for his thirtieth birthday. On that day he became the youngest top manager in the company, where he had started working right after graduating from Columbia University Business School. In a fairly short time, he had made a dizzying career. The son of immigrants who came to America at the age of fourteen, Joseph was among the elite managers of the United States. And it was very impressive indeed.

Finally, a sign appeared ahead informing him that the airport was only a few miles away. In the distance, he could see huge airliners landing and taking off at short intervals. Joseph breathed a sigh of relief.

The phone rang. Slowing down a little, the man pressed the answer button.

- Hello, Mom, I'm listening.

- Joseph, dear, do you manage to get there on time? I'm so worried.

- Don't worry, Mom, I'm trying. I'll call you later.

- Cheers, dear.

At thirty-three, Joseph was still unmarried. Parents were upset because, in a normal Jewish family, children were supposed to get married in time, that is, at the age of twenty-two or twenty-three. Joseph had a girlfriend, but no hint of a serious relationship.

It was fifteen minutes before the end of check-in, and he had to park his car in time.

Ten minutes later, Joseph was hurrying through the registration hall with his sports bag on his shoulder, followed by a porter pushing a stroller with a large suitcase, barely able to keep up. The check-in counter was empty, and the employees wearily glanced at the clock to close the check-in and leave. The porter hurried over to them, dumped the suitcase on the scales, and Joseph put his passport and ticket in front of the bored receptionist.

- You're late, mister, he said with a pleasant smile.

- Oh, sorry, such terrible traffic, answered Joseph in an apologetic tone.

- Have a nice flight!

- Thank you so much. And have a nice day! - The man could barely catch his breath after the crazy race. Always busy, he had miscalculated his time and left the house too late.

At that moment Joseph thought of his parents and called them back. They were already pre-retirement, and he had bought a small house for them in Florida, where they had spent nearly three seasons, moving to their New York apartment in the summer. Despite his tremendous busyness, Joseph tried to keep his parents in his orbit at all times.

Forty minutes later he boarded the Boeing, where he was greeted by a pretty flight attendant. He entered the first-class cabin, sat in a comfortable chair, and stretched his legs.

As soon as the plane took off, the flight attendants bustled around the passengers, offering them soft and strong drinks. Joseph ordered a whiskey, wanting to relieve himself of the day's stress. Taking a sip of the cool moisture, he felt a pleasant rush of warmth in his chest and finally relaxed. His eyelids became heavy and closed on their own. He fell asleep.

This was the first time Joseph had flown to Russia (that's what people in America still called the former Soviet Union) since his family had emigrated from Baku to the United States almost twenty years earlier. Over the past fifteen years, unimaginable changes had taken place in the part of the world to which Joseph's plane was taking him, namely, the collapse of the country, devastation, war, economic collapse, and famine. It seemed that the people of the former Soviet Union, clutched in the grip of monstrous circumstances and given the "freedom" that was not deserved by them, perceived it as permissiveness and turned their eyes to each other. Neighbor against neighbor. Overnight, the old comrades became enemies, recalling past grievances to one another. Joseph watched this madness from another part of the world and could not believe his own eyes and ears.

In the early nineties, Armenian refugees from Baku began emigrating to America. Joseph met some of the families, and they told him horrific stories from their lives. Having lived in this city until he was fourteen, Joseph refused to believe them; it was too difficult for him to imagine that Azerbaijanis were capable of such inhuman cruelty. They told him how a frenzied mob had broken into apartments and murdered, thrown people alive off balconies, cut off their heads, and raped women. "How is it possible...? - Joseph repeated to himself. - No, it's just unbelievable!"

He knew the whole story of the conflict over Nagorno-Karabakh and the events in Sumgait and Baku only by hearsay, from Armenians, and from Russian-language newspapers published in New York. He was not able to meet and talk with Azerbaijanis: there were too few of them in this city.

Back in 1987, Joseph tried to call his old friends from the Soviet Union for the first time, but none of the numbers answered or were disconnected.

Where is Armen now? Even the Russians were said to have escaped from Azerbaijan. Where is Volodya...?

Chapter 2

Joseph was born in the ancient city of Baku, located on the shores of the Caspian Sea, which has retained the historic buildings of its time of formation to this day.

Icheri-Sheher ("inner city") is rightfully called the Baku Acropolis, which immerses visitors into deep antiquity. This living legend, a subject of national pride, is the heart of Baku. Ancient fortress walls were founded in the second century AD and embedded far into the sea, and the waves of the gray Caspian Sea crashed against their impregnable stone firmness. The future capital of Azerbaijan started from a territory of 22 hectares surrounded by fortress buildings.

Over time, the water receded, and in place of the drained area stretched a huge, almost five kilometers, the famous and beautiful Seaside Boulevard, one of the largest boulevards in Europe.

The fortress walls, towers with loopholes, Maiden's Tower, and the remained parts of the palaces - all these traces of the glorious past have survived to the present day. Almost all narrow and crooked streets of Icheri-Sheher, where two people can not pass each other, are covered with paving stones, old two- and three-storey houses of two centuries ago, almost touching the balcony, and you can easily walk from one house to another. This is exactly the landscape typical of the so-called Fortress, as the Russian-speaking people of Baku call the historic part of the city. It hides like a precious pearl in the womb of a huge shell of the modern megapolis, nestled on the sea brink. There is peace and quiet here, the city transport can not enter here. Life slows down its pace, getting as if in a parallel dimension, and the tall silent walls with empty eyes protect this place from the invasion of civilization.

Another Baku landmark, the so-called European part of the city, was built thanks to the oil boom of the late 19th and early 20th centuries. It was built by Italian and Russian architects using the money of local and Western magnates. Sharp architectural contrast between the Eastern antiquity of the fortress and the European style of the new quarter gave Baku a unique identity and always struck the imagination of tourists. The European part as if gradually surrounded the inner old fortress massif from three sides.

Subsequent urban planning was associated with the construction of buildings of the Soviet era, declaring monumentalism and disfiguring the architectural harmony of Baku.

The latest to be constructed were buildings of post-Soviet construction, which were single-type high-rises, haphazardly spotted across the cityscape and reinforcing the effect of architectural chaos.

Joseph was born in one of the houses located in the European part of the city. The building was built in the nineties of the 19th century. It was originally a three-storey house, but after World War II, in 1947, a fourth floor was added on top. Before the revolution, the house belonged to one of the oil magnates. It was said that it was Nobel himself. Later it was expropriated and given to the people.

The ceilings on the first and second floors were five meters high, and on the third floor, they were reduced to four meters. The walls on the first floor were one and a half meters thick and were also gradually thinner on the upper floors. A special mixture of raw egg white, beer, and sand was used in the construction of the house, which was made of large, well-rounded river pebbles. This unusual mix gave it a particular strength so that it celebrated its centenary and was not about to stop there. The unique materials and a well-thought-out plan helped to ensure that the apartments were always warm in winter and cool in summer. Today, the inhabitants of the house enjoy gorgeous fireplaces tiled with multicolored tiles and original stucco decorations of angels and roses on the walls and ceilings. The facade of the house was also elaborately decorated and made a great impression. The entrance to the courtyard was in the form of a large arch with a monogram on top, the house's emblem. The beautifully patterned iron gates were always locked at night.

However, all this pomposity quickly evaporated as soon as you got through the arch into the courtyard. Here, right along the arched wall, were big ugly black garbage bins where vile rodents rustled with rotting paper at night. Those who were afraid of rats had to literally run through the place. Then the archway ended, and a large courtyard appeared.

Courtyards of this type were called "Italian Courtyards" for some reason. It was said that exactly the same ones were built in Italy, but I could hardly believe it. Enfilades of huge halls were rearranged and divided by numerous communal partitions, in which an unknown number of people were huddled. There were open, communal balconies on all floors, stretching in a circular manner. There was always laundry hanging on the thrown ropes from the second to the fourth floor. The residents of the first floor, who did not have balconies, hung laundry right in the middle of the indoor area, which prevented the local kids from running and playing freely. There were a lot of people, all poor, but they lived honestly and cheerfully. The only occasional trouble was between neighbors or a drunken husband and an unfaithful wife, which in no way overshadowed the overall cheerful atmosphere.

The local kids loved to scurry around the yard, all over the balconies, and even on the roof. Angry women and men always grumbled at the noisy, happy tomboys.

The inseparable friends Rafik, Armen, Volodya, and Joseph were among them. They were all born here and began to be friends as soon as they learned to walk and talk. Such companies were very typical for Baku in general - the whole city had the reputation of being super-international. The old generation of Soviet people probably remembers the existence of such a strange nation as "the Baku people," although in those days no one thought about the concept of "nation" and "nationality. Everything was common, Soviet. The four little friends in the yard were nicknamed musketeers.

- Here come the musketeers! - The younger kids shouted after them. The friends went to a school close to home and they were in the same class. As usual, there were also "elite" groups of 4 - 5 girls and boys. Of course, the "musketeers" were among them, too, and they dominated the whole class. The boys courted the "elite" girls, and all the other "ordinary" classmates cried over the boys' antics. Usually, after choosing the object of bullying, sadistic scenes began with the inherent unknowing cruelty of children.

One of the victims of the Musketeers was a girl named Nadia. The boys called her Nadya Piggy, because at the age of twelve she was quite a big and fat girl, in comparison to which her friends seemed like baby birds. She was a head taller and twice as big as they were. She was a mountain of white meat. Her face was like the fattened snout of a young piglet. She bore a striking resemblance to this animal in the shape of her nose, which was much hooked and turned up, the pouty little lips full of blood, the cheeks plump as if they were always full of food, and the head, almost perfectly round, which was crowned with two red bows like two protruding ears. Her smile exposed her large, white, crooked teeth. Nadia must have suffered from some kind of sexual pathology. In her young years she, like a drug addict, needed the touch of a boy's hands and was not childishly melted by their affection. Having detected such tendencies in Nadya, the boys literally devoted every break to her. Five or six boys, like furious dogs, pounced on the girl, playing the role of a wounded and hunted animal, and pushed her to the far corner of the classroom. There they pinned her down on all sides. All this was accompanied by shouting and screaming, Nadya was biting wildly and resisting as best she could. If she succeeded in throwing the boys off her like puppies, the hounding started. In the end, Nadya was huddled behind a coat rack by the back wall. The coat rack simply slaving away under the weight of the students' outerwear, and when six or seven people squeezed behind it, it shook every time, threatening to collapse. The girl would crouch in the corner and, exhausted, crawl down slowly, squatting and spreading her knees wide. She threw her head back, rolled her eyes, calmed down, and a blissful smile appeared on her face. The children's hands were eagerly scrambling between her legs, trying to bring her and themselves some real pleasure.

All this lasted a few minutes. Then the bell sobered up the little devils, and one by one they jumped out from behind the coat rack. Nadya was the last to come out, of course, with a different expression on her face: happy and confident, her cheeks were as red as a ripe tomato. Nadya was totally indifferent to who came at her, so the "musketeers" sometimes invited the boys from other classes to hunt her. They did everything they could, what their childish mind could get up to, what nonsense they could do! It's hard for adults to understand it all... Human memory is short and often erases memories of what happened in childhood. But for children such fun was normal, something as a matter of course. And the more daring the children's antics, the more influential they seemed to themselves.

The happy childhood of the seventies passed unnoticed. Real adult life with its problems passed by, because the "Musketeers" were just teenagers. Just sometimes they would catch a scene with their parents fighting behind the wall, arguing about money and the fact that some "could live a normal life" and some "dragged out a miserable existence.

The families of the friends had different levels of material well-being, but this did not interfere with their communication. Volodya lived with his mother, and the others had two parents each. The boy did not do well in school, and his teachers did not recommend him to enter the ninth grade, believing that he would not be able to master the program. Volodya himself did not want to do that either. He planned to go to a construction college and start working for a living in two years. His mother's salary was barely enough to make ends meet.

The other guys were doing well and were going to continue their studies at school. All four were upset about the upcoming changes since they were used to spending most of the day together. But more serious tests awaited them ahead.

The news of Joseph and his family's departure for Israel came out of the blue. It was so unexpected that at first, the friends did not even pay much attention to it. They didn't understand what immigration is and what Israel had to do with it, since it was only 1981. In Baku, the emigration wave that began in the Soviet Union in 1977 was low, almost unique. The green light was turned on after the General Secretary of the Central Committee of the Communist Party of the Soviet Union Leonid Brezhnev in Helsinki signed a document authorizing Soviet Jews to move to Israel for permanent residence. The Soviet children had never heard of this, except, of course, for Joseph, who had given his parents his word not to tell anyone, not even the Musketeers, until the very end. They frightened their son that otherwise they might all be imprisoned. Being a very obedient boy, Joseph kept quiet.

He revealed his secret to his friends just ten days before his departure. The reaction was very mixed. The guys started joking: "Look, you're going abroad, so take our orders... But when Joseph explained that, like other Jews, he was leaving the Soviet Union forever and there was no way back, they were shocked. Baku did not have the same moods that took place in Moscow, Leningrad, Kyiv, Minsk, or even Tbilisi. The dissident intelligentsia, chatting in their kitchens, was so limited in number that it could not be compared to the capitals of the other Soviet republics.

The dumbfounded children could not comprehend what was going on. Where was Joseph going? Why? What would he do there, and how would they live without him, and he without them? Just a little more than a week left. Joseph's parents were afraid of rumors and unnecessary hype, so they arranged the good-bye dinner in the narrowest circle.

When the Musketeers arrived at the doorstep of Joseph's apartment, relatives and friends of the family had already gathered. The guys were in a completely different world, where all that could be heard was talk about who had already left the Soviet Union and who was just about to leave. Everyone congratulated the newly minted emigrants on their good luck and thought they were lucky to get their exit permits in a relatively short period of time.

Volodya felt so sick at heart from all this talk that he invited Joseph out for a walk, moreover that it was a relatively warm and quiet April evening.

Once outside, the boys walked toward the boulevard. Buds were swelling on all the trees and bushes, and spring scents were in the air.

- I don't understand - why, what for? I don't know why. And where? Israel! It's hot there, only desert, camels, and thorns," Volodya said indignantly.

Burdened with guilt and in some way a sense of betrayal, Joseph tried not to argue, not to prove anything, and only calmed his friend, trying to reduce the pain of the impending separation.

- Yes, you are right... But my father's relatives, who live there, wrote him that it's not so bad...

- "It's not so bad"? So, if that's the case, you have to go...? Leave your home, the town you were born in, your friends with whom you shared bread and salt, joy and sorrow?! - Vova was about to burst into tears.

Suddenly, Joseph could not stand it and began to cry. Clasping his face in his hands, he sobbed out loud. And Volodya, with his eyes rounded, stared at him in confusion. Rafiq hugged his friend and sharply told Vladimir:

- Can't you see he's not himself? Don't you notice your friend's condition at all? Why are you pushing him? - Then he turned to Joseph. - All right, Joseph, calm down, you know Vova.

Still sobbing, the teenager wiped his tears with his hand and hugged Rafik too.

- Come on, I am not offended! It was just all so much pressure... I couldn't stand it.

After a minute of silence he went on:

- Honestly, I also did not expect that everything would turn so quickly and abruptly. I'm upset, too, that I'm losing everything here, that I'm going into the unknown, and it's always scary.

- Are we at a funeral or what?! Come on, guys, - Armen said cheerfully, trying to cheer up his friends.

- And this is worse than a funeral, - insisted Vova. - At funerals, we bury the dead, and here we say goodbye to the alive.

- Will you finally shut up, or not? - Armen sharply interrupted Vova.

- Guys, it seems like you know each other for the first day! Thank God, it's been fourteen years! All things work out for the best. Joseph's leaving, and he's going to start a new life. That's interesting. The only thing I regret is that we won't be able to communicate because of the "Iron Curtain", - Armen philosophically summed up.

- What curtain? - Vova asked.

- The iron curtain! You have to listen to the Voice of America and the BBC! - proudly inserted his friend.

- Nope! They make up all kinds of nonsense, - said Volodya incredulously.

- He's an ideologue person, he doesn't listen to enemy voices, said Rafik with a chuckle.

- Come on, and what's not enough for you? You keep thinking about overseas. You're going mad from fat! - grumbled Vova.

- Well, yeah, no matter how much you feed the wolf, he still looks into the woods, - Armen grinned and blinked at Rafik.

- Enough, guys! - Vova grudgingly exclaimed and turned away offensively.

- Guys, let's calm down! There are only a few days left. And we need to spend them in a way to make them long remembered. Who knows, when we'll meet again... - said Armen.

Joseph's parents, Marik and Mila, had a lot of organizational things to take care of: getting various certificates, arranging the rent of the apartment and paying for its future repairs, getting visas, ordering tickets, selling something... And packing, packing, packing... They were leaving, abandoning their past, the country they thought they belonged to, their professional life with its many happy days. They were leaving behind relatives and friends they had made during the years of study and work, and the graves of their parents. They left behind beloved things and books. They were leaving, not knowing what lay ahead. Into the unknown.

The last week flew by like a blink of an eye.

Then it was Vienna, Rome, and New York. They found themselves in a different reality. Since then, Joseph never heard from his friends.

Chapter 3

Like all Soviet Jews who emigrated to Israel at that time, Joseph and his parents first arrived in the capital of Austria. An Israeli representative met them at the airport and explained that they could fly to their country the next day. Then Marik revealed to the envoy the true intention of his family: they would be waiting for permission from relatives in the United States to enter.

When they arrived, they boarded a minibus that passed through the airport and drove into a large park. People were jogging in the alleys on both sides of the driveway, some riding bicycles, and some riding horses in old-fashioned costumes. Next to the car, a mare darted by, harnessed to a horse-drawn carriage, where a couple in love were hugging each other. Children ran along the meadows and lawns with their mothers or nannies and governesses sitting on fancy benches.

The park ended and the minibus continued driving through the beautiful and clean streets, where the well-dressed and lively crowd walked leisurely, without any fuss. Mila and Marik, who had never been abroad, were sitting like mesmerized, staring out of the window.

They drove for quite a long time. Finally, they arrived at the guesthouse "Korkius" on Haacken-gasse.

The room was on the second floor. The room was big, with three beds, a bathroom, a refrigerator, a gas stove, pots, pans, tablecloths, dishes, and cutlery. Looking around, Mila unintentionally exclaimed:

- Thank God for letting us escape! Thanks to Brezhnev for not objecting to letting the Soviet Jews go!

Here they had several days to stay. The next evening Joseph's family decided to walk around the city. Many of the stores were already closed, but even looking at the windows made Marik and Mila feel half-shocked.

They returned to the guesthouse around midnight. They got up early in the morning, dressed lightly according to the weather, and drove to the market.

The square in front of the entrance was full of flowers. When they entered the roofed building, Marik and Mila were frozen in amazement. They were used to the lavish luxury of Azerbaijani markets, and nothing could surprise them. However, they had never seen anything like this before. Baskets of strawberries, raspberries, and cherries were scarlet on the counters despite the season. Bundles of clouded grapes dangled nearby, and mountains of bananas, oranges, and grapefruits loomed. Proudly displaying their bunched-up firm green leaves, there were orange and yellow ripe pineapples. Rows of vegetables were bursting beneath the piles of greens. Tomatoes, cucumbers, eggplant, lettuce, and fresh mushrooms were arrayed in fanciful combinations.

For some time, the couple couldn't get over this year-round abundance. However, the biggest shock awaited them in the meat section. Marik saw meat of all varieties lying and hanging, with and without bones, cleaned and scraped, plucked and gutted chickens, ducks, and geese. For several minutes the man was speechless, staring at the red-and-pink picture that seemed unreal as if it had come from a Flemish painter's painting. Leaving the market, they hurried back as their time to visit HIAS, a Jewish charity organization that helps Soviet Jews emigrate, approached. They were greeted with a warm welcome as if they had been expected for a long time. After a conversation, they helped them fill out the paperwork and were told that they would be leaving for Rome in a day. After receiving envelopes with money, the family went to a guesthouse.

The next day was their last day in Vienna, and they decided to see St. Stephen's Cathedral, the patron saint of the capital, located in the old part of the city. They saw the church shining with golden colors, its towers reaching up to the sky, and its sloping roof lined with golden tiles. Baroque style adjoined the architectural solution with arrow-shaped Gothic, and this eclecticism gave the cathedral a cheerfulness and airy lightness.

The interior furnishings were astonishingly luxurious-not garish, but noble, keeping dignity. For lack of time, they could not stay to admire every painting, sculpture, aisle decoration, and chancel, but they still went up the stairs of the south tower, climbing three hundred and forty-three steps. From here they had an unforgettable view of the evening city, glittering with lights of every imaginable and inconceivable color as if a festive illumination had been switched on in honor of their arrival. This was how they remembered the beautiful capital.

In the morning they packed their belongings, got into the minibus, and drove to the train station.

A representative from HIAS met the departing passengers on the platform and handed them their tickets. Everyone got into their train carriages. The train traveled along the railroad in the Alps. The migrants in the adjoining compartments crowded around the windows in the corridor, with the windows rolled down, gazing out at the Alpine villages and the marvelous mountain scenery below. The air was delightful - fresh but not cold.

After traveling halfway across Italy from north to south, the group arrived in Rome, where they were met by HIAS staff again. Special buses took the guests to prepared apartments.

The next day, Marik's family went to the charity's office, where they were given the documents to get visas to enter the United States and were explained how they could cash the check they had been given.

Now, the eternal city of Rome was in front of them. Marik froze in front of the Colosseum, the largest of the ancient Roman amphitheaters, which had been constructed in a hollow between the Esquilino, Palatine, and Caelian hills, on the very spot where the pond that had once belonged to Nero's Golden House had been located. The Colosseum stood out from all similar constructions of the time for the sheer enormity of its size:

The length of its outer ellipse was 524 meters; the length of the major axis was 188 meters; the length of the minor axis was 156 meters; the arena was 86 meters long and 54 meters wide; the height of the walls varied from 48 to 50 meters. With these parameters, the Colosseum could accommodate up to 87,000 spectators! Marik could not have imagined even in his dreams that the day would come when he could touch these ancient stones with his own hands.

- Mila, did you ever imagine that you would be in Rome? - He asked his wife excitedly.

- See, even the most daring dreams come true," replied the smiling wife.

There were three families - eleven people in total - awaiting their fate. Each family received a room. They shared the kitchen, two bathrooms, and the balcony. In the evenings the whole company would sit on the balcony and talk. This place was nicknamed "the dime." The news came here before the White House, the Kremlin, or the Knesset.

- We should go to Detroit, declared Motya from Minsk with aplomb. - Ford factories need our workforce!

- And I'll be waiting for Canada, - argued the boxing coach from Kyiv.

- I was advised to go to Australia, - the butcher from Berdychev intervened.

- Who advises you to go to Australia? - Yasha, the joker from Vitebsk, asked.

- My wife, - he smiled embarrassedly.

- I'm not married, Yasha answered, but I know from my friends' experience that you should listen to your wife. They say in Australia, every newly arrived family is given two kangaroos right away!

But the butcher was humorless.

- Yasha, he inquired, is kangaroo meat good?

He had no time to answer because Lazarus appeared on the threshold, and the eyes of everyone turned in his direction. This man had an advantage over the other emigrants: He was being welcomed by a third cousin from Chicago. Lazarus had never seen her, but he was full of family feelings and called her nothing less than "my dear sister Rose".

- Lazarus, what do they write from Chicago? - Yasha called out to him.

- My dear sister is very busy: family, business.

- And what is their business?

- Yasha, not them, but her! It's a big factory. It's called "LAUNDROMAT".

- And what is it? - The butcher inquired.

- Apparently, Lazarus really needs the money. Rose, come in! said Yasha with a chuckle. - And then the last three letters...

- That's not how you should spell it, - objected Lara, an accountant from Moscow.

- But it's how you hear it! - insisted wit.

Everyone laughed, but Lazarus let the joke pass:

- Yasha, a woman leading a business - it's... you know what...

But as soon as I get there, I'll put everything on the right track.

- You're a good brother, Lazarus, - said Yasha with a smile. A Candidate in Sciences from Riga joined the conversation:

- How hard do you think it will be to find a job in my field? I'm a geneticist.

- If you really want it, you will find it, - Yasha said assuredly.

- And I want to go to Georgia, said Givi from Tbilisi. - I'll go to work in a restaurant, I can even wash dishes or clean the floor. It doesn't matter. Then I'll introduce them to our Georgian cuisine - they'll love it! They'll give me a job as a chef. And then I'll open my own restaurant.

- Sounds great, Givi! - Yasha patted him on the shoulder. - I'm ready to book a table at your restaurant!

- If they raise kangaroos there, it means that their meat is tasty after all, the butcher from Berdychiv kept talking. - I should have gone straight to Australia. I would have been already rich.

Thus, unnoticed, with mixed feelings, almost a month flew by. On the one hand, these people were euphoric about being in the beautiful city of Rome, and on the other, they experienced a humiliating feeling of complete uncertainty about the future. It was a feeling familiar to hundreds of migrants staying in the Italian capital. Some could not stand it and left for Canada or Australia. One day Marik, Mila, and Joseph went to the American Consulate for an interview.

In the designated office, where they were invited to go, the guests were greeted by an official who spoke fluent Russian. He was very friendly, asked various questions related to Marik's professional activities and American relatives, and at the end of the interview, he announced a positive decision. A sense of joy filled their anxious souls, and Mila even cried with happiness.

Soon it was the last day in Rome. The next morning, they left from Leonardo da Vinci International Airport for New York.

Chapter 4

In New York, they were met by Marik's third cousin, Leonid, who lived at the famous Brighton Beach Street, considered the center of America's Russian-speaking emigration, with his wife and daughter. It was shown on Soviet television by Professor Zorin, a popular political commentator at the time. The dumbfounded Soviet viewers were shown stalls stocked with food and fat saleswomen posing for the cameras. The most indelible impression on the unsophisticated citizens was the enormous variety of sausage products. Of course, Zorin showed a homeless person peacefully resting on the ground, and broken glass in the window of some abandoned building, but no one focused their attention on this.

Leonid rented a two-room apartment next door for his relatives and even furnished it with some furniture. Before the tired newcomers had time to realize it, he dragged them for a walk along Brighton Beach Avenue. As he walked, Marik's brother waved his arms and shook his head so vigorously, explaining and showing them something, as if he wanted to pour out all the information, he knew on the poor guests' minds on the first day.

The five-story house where Joseph and his parents had moved in was a prewar building. A spacious hallway lined with beautiful tiles, mirrored walls, large floor vases with artificial flowers, and marble shelves with pots of live plants - everything shone in perfect cleanliness, not a single speck of dirt was visible on the floor.

In New York, Joseph's family was under the tutelage of NYANA, a prominent American Jewish organization that taught English, introduced American laws, and helped the family to adapt to the new world. The organization helped the family with furniture and even provided them with their first winter outerwear. The settlers got free rides on city transportation, breakfast, and lunch while they studied. The municipal welfare office also paid a monthly cash allowance for food, clothing, and part of the rent. Marik's family was eligible for free medical care and could get very expensive medications at no cost. Joseph's parents were in lasting shock at all the happiness and comfort that had so suddenly descended upon them.

Often they were surprised to meet former compatriots in Brighton with dissatisfied faces and could not understand what could have caused it. In response to their questions, they usually heard exclamations that "when you've lived here as long as we have, you will suffer because of the same shit. Many emigrants were nostalgic for their past lives, and they didn't even like the local food. Everything was tasteless, not like it was at home like they were used to.

Marik and Mila resented the unfair position of the former Soviet citizens toward the country that gave them shelter and where they were so eager to go. On the other hand, it was also understandable, from a purely human point of view: they had come here at a mature age, having lived most of their lives in a country with a completely different mentality. Their youth, careers, and friends were in the past, and now it was as if they were locked in a golden cage, cut off from the usual communication, whatever it was.

So, caught in the maelstrom of fast-paced New York life, Joseph and his parents floundered in it as hard as they could to avoid drowning. The main goal of their existence was to get back on their feet. On the one hand, the harsh conditions in this country were not so fatal, but on the other hand, starting a business was not that easy, for the competition was fierce. The harshness of the conditions, paradoxically, was due to the ample opportunities that existed in the American social system. Equal start-up opportunities were encouraged and created fierce competition among those willing to take advantage of them, and healthy competition set the tone for American life. The great lure of the real attainment of material goods drove millions of people on this continuous labor conveyor belt that could lead to the cherished dream. This is what the greatness of American democracy was built on, because in the end, the most deserving people managed to make their way to success.

At the time of his emigration, Marik was forty-three years old. The most uncomfortable age for changes: no longer young, but not yet old. The main problem for migrants in this age group was the language barrier. English was so damn slow to learn, foreign words wouldn't settle in mind. The six-month course had come to nothing. Existing solely on an allowance was uncomfortable and humiliating, as well as unbearable, given the many temptations around us.

It was something that Marik and no one else had to solve. One cannot say that emigration changed people in any way; perhaps it just broke them. But basically, the way you were in your homeland was the way you stayed here. Emigration only brought out the forces that everyone had, destructive or creative. Success in finding a job came to those who were able to find a compromise between their ambitions and real opportunities.

Realistically assessing his chances, Marik decided to work as a cab driver, as did many middle-aged and elderly Soviet migrants. At first, he felt a twinge: after all, the chief engineer of the plant had suddenly become an ordinary driver. However, when he met his new colleagues from the limousine company, it became clear that his feelings were not unique: all these people shared the same situation - and there was nothing he could do about it. In fact, his colleagues were a professor, a former school principal, a pianist, and a geologist.

Gradually Marik accepted the situation, but he never got used to the hourly feeling of humiliation that any migrant experiences in a new place. He told himself that he had to endure it and, perhaps, it would get easier with time. For this, he strained all his will. There was no other way. After all, he saw many others around him who broke down, unable to endure the ordeal. As a result, among Russian-speaking newcomers, there were a huge number of divorces and nervous breakdowns. Men often drank themselves to death, women left negligent spouses who had become a burden, and tried to marry Americans.

Marik was envious of the people of this country, of those self-confident, self-sufficient individuals who felt like they owned the place. Like the ugly duckling in the fairy tale, he longed to be a part of this life, to enter their circle. But between them lay a huge linguistic and social gap. More and more often the man recalled the words of an ancient Greek poet: "For full happiness, a man must have a glorious fatherland.

In time Marik began to grow accustomed to freedom. It was pleasant and comfortable to live in America. However, he noticed that many migrants had never let go of homesickness. He even had a theory about it. He believed that having made the fateful step, these people showed the strength of their character, but involuntarily took a piece of the Soviet Union with them. Marik saw the solution to the problem as forgetting the past. And only then would one be truly free.

Marik loathed people who mocked the religious feelings and traditions of other nations. He believed that the greatness of a country and society was not about being outraged by, for example, Muslim women wearing burqas or Hasidic women wearing wigs, but rather that people should be able to dress and live according to their traditions without fearing for their lives and reputations, but in accordance with the law. This was the case in the multicultural, multilingual conglomerate known as New York, where everyone was allowed to be themselves: to wear hijabs, paisas, funny cylinder hats, wigs, beards, shorts, and miniskirts. In the U.S. human beings feel less alien than anywhere else in the world.

Marik and Mila were very happy with Joseph's school progress. At school, as in any social structure in the United States, there was a clear stratification. Among the pupils, this was expressed, above all, in the complexity of the curriculum. For example, there were classes for students whose native language was not English, intermediate-level classes, and so-called "advanced" classes with extremely complicated programs and many extracurricular activities. The children were put into the relevant categories according to their level of knowledge and mental abilities. In this way no one was left out and, most importantly, the dignity of the children was not undermined. The students in each class had roughly the same level of development.

The Soviet educational system was certainly more intense and exacting than that in the United States, and most students got good knowledge. However, there was the same curriculum for top scorers, good scorers, and bad scorers that triggered the mechanism of social-psychological stratification. An "F" student was considered a second or third sort, an egregious bully, almost an outcast-all because he or she got a "D" or "C" in math or Russian. This crippled many children and left a lifelong imprint on their psyche. In addition, the Soviet system did not take into account the human qualities of the students. It was not always the case that the moral character of an "F" student was worse than that of an "A" student. But nobody cared about that. Knowledge, numbers, and discipline were paramount in a growing individual. In the United States, even the weakest student in a class consisting of immigrants felt quite happy, for no one and nothing diminished his dignity. He was in the same position as his fellow students. In the USSR, at parent-teacher meetings, teachers publicly stomped on some students and exalted others. In the United States, the parent-teacher meeting was a confidential meeting between the teacher and the parents and the student, because human dignity and respect were and are paramount.

Joseph was in the most advanced class in Brooklyn's most advanced school, and his progress was impressive. His teachers couldn't stop praising him, and they predicted a bright future for him.

America is truly an amazing country. What is its fundamental difference from most other countries in the world? First and foremost, its absolute diversity, which makes it stand out from multi-level uniformity of the socialist countries. If one realizes this fundamental difference, all the arguments about the poor quality of the U.S. education system fall away. Education here covers all scales from "very bad" to "very good," from immigrant schools to prestigious private educational institutions of world renown. And so it is with everything. You could say that America reflects the diversity of the modern world. That's why they are so relaxed about criticism because you can always find something very good and something very bad. The same laws apply to everyone, so people feel safe, and most people live in well-being and prosperity. Within the law, anything is possible, from vulgar free sex propaganda to the high moral foundations of a conservative segment of society, from sheer human stupidity to the most extraordinary manifestations of human genius. And most importantly - if anyone wishes, every citizen can find a niche for personal expression here, regardless of the level of knowledge, abilities, tastes, and preferences. In this respect, New York is the clearest example of the American way of life. Here all kinds of cultures, arts, history, and religion, all the best and worst features of human civilization coexist in close symbiosis.

This is something Marik often thought about while taking passengers from Brighton Beach to other parts of New York City. This street had become almost native to him. It was not remarkable by itself. Over a great part of it, like a huge serpent, hung an iron, rattling monster called the American subway. Trains still rode on this pile of rusted metal from a century ago, and the horrible metallic rattle was always painful to the eardrums. It was a torture Marik never got used to. All of Brighton was literally silenced by the screeching and rumbling, and it was almost useless to talk. Considering that trains in New York City run strictly on a schedule every five to ten minutes, one could easily imagine the noisy background in which this merry neighborhood lived and still lives.

One of the attractions of the street was its veggie and grocery stores. Here you could buy almost anything sold in all fifteen republics of the Soviet Union.

The people of Brighton themselves were also an important attraction. Not for nothing was it nicknamed Little Odessa, which emphasized the superiority of the Odessa people, who felt that they were the real masters here. It was they who wrested this gracious spot from the African-American contingent and turned the once-criminal neighborhood into a blooming paradise where the Russian-speaking newcomers lived so comfortably. Some former Odessans believed that other immigrants from the Soviet Union had come here for "all ready-made" and were only unfairly reaping the benefits of others. So they used to say to every newcomer, especially if he was not from Odessa, "We've had shit here, and you should have it too."

Brighton has become a pilgrimage destination for visitors and tourists, including because of the beautiful beach. A favorite promenade for Brightoners and visitors is the famous boardwalk, which is a wooden deck that stretches along the ocean shore for several kilometers.

Cozy gazebos and several famous restaurants overlooking it made this place indispensable for entertainment and rest. Some people, taking care of their health, jog on the wooden deck along the shoreline from 6 am, others just stroll, others sit on the benches and breathe the clean ocean air, and still, others prefer to go to a cafe or restaurant to admire the play of small waves and enjoy the light breeze. In the evening, the lanterns are lit, and the relaxed, festive crowd goes out to see and be seen. The courteous waiters skillfully serve the tables in waiting for the visitors. There is live music on holidays and sometimes on weekends, and everyone can dance.

The most amazing sight for the former Soviet people was the fireworks show that could be seen from the boardwalk every Sunday at nine o'clock in the evening. Two warships began firing their cannons, painting astonishingly beautiful colored figures of fire in a black sky strewn with stars, sometimes scattering and sometimes assembling into a bizarre pattern. For Soviet immigrants, fireworks were always associated with some kind of big holiday, but here it was a regular weekly ritual. In a word, when you went to a boardwalk, you got to a celebration of life. People temporarily forgot about work, problems, and illnesses, relaxed and just had carefree fun.

How quickly time flies in America! Many newcomers complain that the days here turn more quickly than in their homeland. Marik was sure that this condition was related to the permanent feeling of stress that all migrants experienced. This subconscious anxiety had become an integral part of their lives, turning into a kind of norm of being. Any person living in the shackles of constant anxiety will feel as if his life is going faster. This is a purely psychological effect.

At first, Marik and his family had to take the subway a lot because it was the most convenient form of public transportation in the city. In New York City, the subway network is extensive. Short and frequent stops, and short (an average of five to fifteen minutes) intervals between trains allow people to get to any point of the giant metropolis relatively quickly. Not for nothing its services are used daily by about six to seven million people.

Marik and his family often took the subway to get to various appointments. The word "appointment" can be included in the Russian language since it is the most used English word among Russian-speaking migrants. It is translated as " scheduled meeting," but the Russian lexical equivalent does not convey the full meaning of the original. In America, no one goes anywhere without a prior appointment. First, you have to call and arrange the day and time of the visit, without that they won't accept you anywhere.

Marik always watched with interest the people sitting and standing around him in the train or carriage (this is the second most popular English word, which is never pronounced here in Russian). People on the subway are usually immersed in their own business, and no one is staring at anyone. Shamelessly staring straight ahead is considered bad manners. That's why Marik looked at everyone furtively.

There's a pretty white girl sitting opposite, immersed in reading a book. Every now and then she sniffs her nose rather loudly, trying not to let the stubborn moisture leak out of her nostril and settle snugly on her pretty upper lip. In the far corner of the wagon, a huge black homeless man, wrapped head to toe in colored clothing, comfortably stretches out on four seats at once. Next to him, right on the floor, is his belongings - an impressively sized black sack filled with unknown junk. The tramp exudes the persistent stench of a rattling mixture of shit, urine, and sweat. That's why the part of the train where he majestically sits is almost empty. The rest is crowded with rows of workers. None of them will disturb his peaceful sleep, they will all just try to stay away from him and occasionally cast a leering glance in his direction when the subtle whiff of the breeze brings the unbearable stench.

There is a common perception that Americans don't like to read. However, this is not entirely true. All subway passengers can be divided into three categories. The biggest of them - people who read newspapers, books, and magazines; the next - people listening to music (with headphones, of course), and finally, those sleeping. Thus, there are practically no idlers among the passengers, gawking idly around.

Another distinguishing feature of the subway is that here, even on a crowded train, no one touches, presses, or pushes anyone with their elbows. And if a wagon is overcrowded, nobody will try to squeeze into it, but will simply wait for the next one. You must agree that these are all elementary things that, perhaps, I shouldn't have written about... But who would argue that it's these little things that cause the most inconvenience?

Sometimes Marik had to drive passengers to Harlem, which is in the northern part of Manhattan. When he first saw the neighborhood in 1983, a treacherous thought flashed through his mind that the whole world was populated by people who were not really culturally developed. The stained sidewalks, the dirt, the piss-smelling entryways, the burned elevator buttons-it was reminiscent of his native Baku and other Soviet cities. The locals, unencumbered by civilization, seemed to have come to enjoy its benefits for a while.

Marik's idle thoughts about the similarities between blacks and Soviets were interrupted by the voice of the dispatcher, who asked him to pick up three boys and take them to an address somewhere near the dispatcher's office. This was in Brooklyn.

As he pulled up to a private house, Marik saw three very young, but very large, African-Americans waiting for him. The noisy youths sprawled carelessly on the seats, took out their cigarettes, and began to fill them with marijuana. Ignoring the driver, the boys talked loudly, gutturally interrupting each other. Marik tried not to notice their antics and was eager to get rid of the not very pleasant passengers as quickly as possible. Soon the whole car filled with smoke, and the pungent, peculiar smell of cannabis hit his nose.

It was a cold January evening, and it was half past nine. Marik rolled down the window to avoid suffocation. He did not yet know the ways very well, and took a wrong turn. One of the passengers in the back, apparently dissatisfied with this, muttered something and lightly knocked the driver on the head. The person in front of him blinked and offered him a drag. Marik shook his head negatively. All three of them laughed in unison, and the man got hit in the head again. The laughter continued. The boys felt their power, and Marik was completely confused. Everything was mixed up in him at that moment - anger, a sense of powerlessness, and humiliation. He was so dazed that he forgot about his walkie-talkie. The man in front of him, as if he had caught his thoughts, grabbed the transmitter and threw it on the back seat. There the device was picked up and, shouting with delight, they hit the driver on the top of the head with it.

Marik couldn't take it anymore, so he started shouting at the young men in a mix of Russian and English. But the guy next to him, noticing his wallet sticking out, began to reach into Marik's pocket. The driver tried to prevent the theft with one hand, but with the other he firmly grasped the steering wheel, continuing to drive. Tears involuntarily spurted from his resentment and helplessness, and, roaring loudly like a hunted animal, he pressed the gas pedal. The car sped off at breakneck speed. The boys, frightened, were quiet at first, and then those in the back asked him to stop. The person in front, disregarding the speed, looked at the driver with shock and muttered:

- Guys, look, he's crying, he's crying...

When finally, Marik stopped not far from the dispatcher's office, the car doors were already open. He did not even think to block them. The three boys jumped out of the car and ran away. Stupefied with anger and humiliation, Marik rushed after them. Soon he caught up with the one sitting next to him. Marik was no good at fighting. He grabbed the boy by the collar with both hands, shook him desperately, and the next minute he was hit in the face with a heavy punch. The fist hit him right in the eyebrow, and with such intensity that it sliced it open. Blood instantly flooded his eye. Marik unclenched his hands, let go of the thief, and automatically grabbed his head. The young man calmly fixed his clothes, turned around, and disappeared into the darkness...

The scar on his eyebrow kept reminding Marik of this unpleasant incident, which almost cost him his right eye. Normally, in such situations, the driver was instructed to leave the car and dial 911 at the first opportunity. But for Marik, as for other newcomers, life in an alien linguistic environment was a great challenge. It had been five years since they had arrived in the United States, and he continued to stutter when speaking to Americans. Marik even drew a parallel between learning English and the man who decided to climb the highest mountain. Full of energy, tirelessly and without rest, he climbs to the top, and it seems as if the peak is very close, literally within arm's reach. In the next moment, his jaw begins to drop, his eyes round in disappointment, and a sense of hopelessness clutches his heart as a new, even more inaccessible height opens up before his eyes. It will require even more effort to overcome. A man takes a deep breath and starts on his way. And now, breathing heavily and barely able to move his legs, he, half-dead but still proud and unbroken, reaches this goal as well. And then his legs finally shake, from anger and helplessness he falls on his knees in despair - in front of him is another mountain, even bigger than the previous one. And so on to infinity. Such a phenomenon is called the "mountain effect," when the victory achieved is in fact only a phantom illusion. Marik had a similar feeling about learning English. The more success he thought he had achieved, the harder the obstacles got in his way.

At home, especially when some disease occurred, Marik often felt insecure and even somehow lonely - and that with numerous, but, alas, not powerful relatives! The fear of a lethal outcome, which could not be prevented by local specialists (for some reason he was so convinced), did not give him any peace. In America, in a completely foreign world, for the first time, he felt safe. Marik trusted American physicians - not so much in their skill as in their conscientiousness. He was not afraid of expensive medical insurance, on the contrary, the high cost was a guarantee of quality treatment. It was because of high-quality therapies that some Canadians preferred to get treatment in the United States. After all, in their home country, where the entire population had government health insurance, one could wait for months for any, even the most minor, procedures.

Perhaps the only thing Marik lacked in New York was an ordinary, quiet and comfortable Baku Street, with its old-fashioned facades, peculiar oriental unkemptness, and an opportunity to make casual conversation with passersby. In New York, this was something unreal, on the verge of fantasy. The crowded flow of people would have dragged the talkers to different ends of the city. There was not that street culture, which was soaked in Baku. A New York Street was just a kind of freeway along which one had to move clearly in the right direction. In Baku, the street was a place of meeting and leisurely conversation.

Undoubtedly, the fate of migrants is difficult, and very often it turns into mental trauma and social insecurity... But the parents' sacrifice is more than paid off by their children!

Marik understood that he would never master English as his native language and would not be able to fully integrate into the American environment, but he was confident that his son Joseph would achieve this.

Chapter 5

At eight o'clock in the evening, Baku time, the plane with Joseph on board landed at Binah International Airport. A man in a border guard uniform entered the business section and said his name loudly. The two of them walked down the stairs and made their way to the airport building. The border guard escorted Joseph to the VIP area, where he was met by a representative of an American company and the local executives. Together they walked down the corridor through the great hall to the outside.

Everything here was new to Joseph. As an unsophisticated teenager, he had left Baku many years ago through the old building and was now back in the city, getting into a modern airport that met all international standards. They got into the Mercedes-Benz, and the car drove them along the familiar road to Baku, twinkling with its lights in the distance.

The guest was lodged at the old "Intourist" hotel. The hotel had been completely renovated and became a five-star hotel. Joseph, who had seen many hotels, was pleasantly surprised by the luxury of the interior. "Wow," he thought, "that's Baku!" They left him to rest, and told him that a car would be arriving at ten o'clock tomorrow morning. After taking a shower, Joseph drank some more whiskey and went to bed.

The next day he had several business meetings, and in the evening, at about six o'clock, he drove up to the house where he was born, and... and was astonished. This building had nothing in common with the one in his memory. Previously black from years of soot and dust, the facade had been whitewashed and gleamed in the sun. The first floor had changed beyond recognition. The windows and shutters had been replaced by darkened showcases reaching down to the ground. Here was the office of some company. The signboard was written in Azerbaijani in Latin letters. Joseph remembered that earlier in Azerbaijan Cyrillic letters were used.

The iron gates had disappeared somewhere. The arch leading to the courtyard was kept perfectly clean, and new green trash garbage cans with lids stood neatly under the canopy. The residents threw out their trash in special cellophane bags. All this left a pleasant impression.

Joseph entered the courtyard. It seemed to him unexpectedly small, though for the children of that time it was so big that it was possible to get lost in it. It was clean, too, and there was no drying laundry hanging over a rope. And most importantly, it was unusually quiet.

The man stood there for a while in confusion. Then he decided to look into Rafik's apartment on the second floor.

He went up the stairs and rang the doorbell. A boy of about twelve opened the door.

- Who do you need?

- I'm actually here to see Rafik...

- Rafik? Rafik who? There is no Rafik.

- Rafik Askerov. Anyway, he used to live here.

- Ah... Hold on. Mom, mom! - the boy shouted and disappeared.

After a while a tall, fat woman in a housecoat appeared.

- What is it? Who do you need?

- The Askerov family used to live here...

- Oh, yes, right... But they moved out a long time ago, about ten or twelve years ago.

- Sorry to bother you, but do you know where they went?

- You know, I still have their address somewhere... I'll see if I can find it. Come in and take a seat. - And she pointed to a chair in the corridor in front of a large mirror.

Joseph didn't recognize this hallway. The new tenants had made a complete renovation.

The woman returned five minutes later.

- Can you believe it, I found it! What a surprise. Usually, you can never find what you need right away. But there you go. The address was in my address book. Here, I've already written it down for you. Look at that! - She went on wondering.

- Thank you very much, Joseph got up from his chair.

- And how do you know them? You do not look like a local, - the lady was interested.

- I came from Moscow, - for some reason Joseph lied. - Rafik and I are friends. Maybe you know a woman Valya and her son Volodya? They lived on the third floor.

- No, I never heard of them before. I don't think there are any such people in our neighborhood. But Aunt Dusya lives on the first floor. She's an old-timer. Ask around, she knows everything and remembers everyone, despite her old age.

- Is Aunt Dusya still alive? - Joseph involuntarily burst out.

- Oh, you know her? - The lady smiled curiously, looking at the guest.

- Yes, I saw her when I visited Rafik, - the man was uncomfortable.

After saying goodbye, Joseph went out into the courtyard and approached Aunt Dusya's apartment. Even her door, walls, and windows were repaired and covered with fresh paint. No one answered the doorbell. Apparently, the woman was not at home.

When Joseph went outside, he decided to go immediately to Rafik's new address. He stopped a passing sixth model of "Zhiguli".

- Where should I drive, boss? - the young boy asked.

He showed him a piece of paper with an address. The young man nodded as he read it.

- You are not local, right? - he inquired in the car.

- Yes, from Moscow, - Joseph decided to lie again.

- For how long?

- A couple of days.

- How is it in Moscow?

- It depends, he answered evasively. All his thoughts revolved around the upcoming meeting.

- It's hard to get a job here. Everything is expensive, and we need to live and feed our children. So I, a person with a university degree, have to steer the wheel to earn a living.

Baku disappointed Joseph. The city turned into a human anthill, which is typical of settlements in the East. The extreme accumulation of people made everything chaotic. Calm and measuredness were gone; all the signs of a bustling, neurotic megalopolis was in evidence. Despite the rapid construction of multistory "boxes", far from oriental architecture, Baku has preserved and increased the oriental atmosphere. Although, perhaps, such a feeling arose in Joseph because of the appearance of most local residents and the streets filled with bazaars, which divided the population into buyers and sellers. As we know, trade had always been of paramount importance in the East. But after religion, of course.

Twenty-five minutes later, Joseph was standing in front of a paneled nine-story building in the fourth microdistrict. Entering the dusty entryway, he climbed the broken stairs to the third floor and rang the bell of apartment number fourteen. An old woman's voice at the door asked in Azerbaijani:

- Who's there?

- This is Joseph Bronstein. We were neighbors in the old courtyard. Rafik and I were friends.

There was silence for a while, then the door slowly opened. A hunched, gray-haired woman stood before Joseph, in whom he could hardly recognize formerly youthful and pretty Maryam-Khanum, Rafik's mother.

"That's what time does to people!" - Joseph gasped in shock.

- Joseph? - the woman repeated quietly. - The same Joseph whose family went to Israel?

- Yes, right, that's me. But not to Israel, to the United States. The woman, hesitating, stepped back, gesturing for the guest to come in.

- How long has it been? I remember you as a boy.

- About eighteen years. I was fourteen at the time.

- Yes, you... you were fourteen years old. And my Rafik was fifteen.

- How is he, where is he now? - Joseph couldn't stand it.

- So you don't know anything? - Maryam-khanum slowly sat down on a chair and looked intently into Joseph's eyes. Tears hung on her eyelashes, and Joseph saw such an expression of sadness and suffering that he involuntarily whispered:

- Is something happened, Aunt Maryam?

- Joseph, darling, our Rafik is gone, we lost him... He died nine years ago, she said quietly, lowering her head and covering her face with her hands.

Joseph's knees buckled and he sat down on a chair nearby. Drops of cold sweat appeared on his forehead, which his right hand unconsciously began to wipe away.

- How... died? - he mumbled. - Where?

- You know nothing? - Maryam-khanum repeated. - It happened during the war, in Karabakh. A year after his death my husband died: my heart couldn't take it. Asya and the child left for Armenia.

- Asya? - Joseph asked again.

- Oh yes, you don't know that either. Rafik and Asya got married.

- And what about Armen?

- Oh, my God! Armen died in the war, too!

At that moment Joseph jumped up, clasped his head with both hands, and, holding back, bellowed:

- "Oh God, what was that for? Why?!

Maryam-hanum slowly got up from her chair, walked over to Joseph, and embraced him. They stood like that for some time together.

- The damned war has taken everything from me...

The old woman approached the portrait of her son hanging on the wall and looked at it for a long time, stroking the curly hair and the smiling face with her hand...

After a while Joseph broke the silence unabashedly:

- Aunt Maryam... It is late. I have to go.

But the distraught mother could see and hear no one but Rafik, her precious child. There he stands before her, smiling slyly as always. Surely, he is going to ask her for something...

Chapter 6

In the morning Rafik was awakened by the loud voice of the Central Television announcer: "Comrade Mikhail Sergeyevich Gorbachev was elected as the General Secretary of the Communist Party of the Soviet Union..."

Rafik had a terrible headache; yesterday he had too much alcohol. The day before he and Armen accompanied Volodya and his mother, who was moving to Rostov-on-Don for permanent residence. Aunt Valya's sister lived there and had long been inviting her relatives to her place. After the swap, they got a two-room apartment in a three-story house. It was sad to say goodbye to another friend, Joseph had left only four years before... And now Volodya was also leaving them. He wanted to drown out his sadness with a lot of alcohol.

It was 1985, and nothing foretold the unpredictable events of the near future. After Gorbachev came to power, Gorbachev set a course for acceleration, and then announced a transparency policy - and the whole country immersed itself in reading previously inaccessible information that had been hidden from the Soviet people for decades. The mass reading binge lasted almost until 1990. Having paid tribute to printed materials, people flocked to television, and not without reason. Sessions of the Supreme Soviet of the Soviet Union began to be broadcast live. For that time it was a grandiose word show, unlike anything the world had ever seen before. People could not believe their ears and eyes. After all, the stunned viewer, without any offense, was poured out a whole stream of previously highly secret facts. It was truly much more interesting than reading books and magazines! People set up TVs at work. Almost no one wanted to attend to their daily business: with jaws and ears hanging back, everyone was watching and listening to the rebellious speeches of people's deputies. Dissident topics that previously Soviet people had been afraid to discuss even in their kitchens began to be officially broached. People were astonished by the bold statements of political scientists, journalists, writers, and deputies.

Where did the fear go? Did anyone realize then that without it it would be impossible for the empire called the Soviet Union to function properly? But the genie was let out of the bottle. We can only guess whether this plan for the collapse of the country had brilliant architects, but the future has shown that the implementation of these plans absolutely failed to live up to expectations. Of course, many stayed in power and became fabulously rich. But it is unlikely that others would have agreed to participate in this adventure if they had known in advance the results.

...As usual, at eight-thirty in the morning, Rafik came out of the building, lit a cigarette, and headed for the courtyard archway. He was a fifth-year student at the University of Construction.

- Hello, Rafik!

Armen's younger sister Asya stood on the balcony of the second floor and waved at him.

- Oh, Asya, good morning! How are you?

- Fine, and you?

- I'm fine, too. Are you going to the university?

Asya was in her third year in the philological department. Tall, with long loose hair, big beautiful green eyes and stunning eyelashes, the young man really liked her. But it was at that moment when Rafik sensed that he didn't just like Asya. It was as if he had been hit by an electric shock, and he realized that he had fallen in love. The boy looked at her and could not take his eyes off her. He seemed to notice something about her he hadn't seen before. He could not explain what it was. That's how love is born...

Apparently, he had a whole range of feelings on his face.

- Rafik, is something wrong? Are you alright? - Asya smiled.

- Yes, sure, I'm fine, I just immersed in thoughts... It happens, doesn't it?

- Of course, it happens! - Asya agreed.

- I'm sorry, but I have to run. I'll see you later, ok?

- Yes, see you later! Bye! - She laughed and waved at him.

The two had long been attracted to each other, but today Rafik definitely and irrevocably lost his mind.

From that moment on, it was as if he had been switched. He wanted to see Asya all the time and to be close to her. The only thing that stopped him was a feeling of embarrassment in front of Armen and his parents. They could easily guess his feelings. Rafik met Armen every day, but he was absent-minded, often lost in himself, withdrawn, and paid little attention to what his friend was saying. But every time they talked about Asya, the boy suddenly changed and could endlessly talk and ask questions about her. Armen only shook his head and grinned without Rafik noticing.

Nearly half a year passed like that. Rafik became absolutely sad. He never allowed himself to get close to Asya. In the Caucasus it was thought that first young people had to get the consent of their relatives and then date the girl. No one knows how long this suffering would have gone on if Armen hadn't decided to have a frank conversation one day. Left alone with his friend, he, stammering and blushing thickly, brought up an exciting topic.

- I want to talk about Asya, he said in a whisper for some reason, and then stared at the ground with his eyes downcast.

- About Asya? What happened? - Rafik also blushed and exclaimed in surprise.

- Nothing is wrong... It seems that she is in love with you.

- With me?! - The man pretended to be a fool and exclaimed. - How could you know that?

- She told me herself.

- Asya told you... She told you...? - Rafik repeated like an echo and became silent. His face and neck were covered with red spots.

- I'm sorry for daring to tell you about it... But you see, she seems to be suffering.

- She's... Suffering? So I... - And Rafik faltered, not knowing how to continue.

Armen came to help him.

- Look, buddy, we've known each other all our lives. And I treat you like my own brother. Tell me, how do you feel about Asya?

- I like Asya very much, but I...

- I understand you. But don't worry about anything. Do whatever your soul tells you to do. And our friendship must not interfere with your relationship.

- Are you blessing us?

- Yes. I am the elder brother, and therefore I have the right. I love you as my closest friend and respect you as a man. Who else but you would I like to be related to!

So Rafik got the green light, and events began to develop rapidly.

Asya's and Armen's father, Suren Sergeyevich, worked in the Baku prosecutor's office and was a respected person. After learning from his wife that their daughter was dating Rafik, he muttered excitedly:

- I think it's too early for her to get married.

- Suren, my darling! Asya is graduating from university next year. It's the right time to get married!

One evening the girl came home late. The light was on in Suren Sergeyevich's home office. Her father's voice was heard from behind the door:

- Asya, is that you?

- Yes, Dad.

- Please come here.

- Hi! Asya came up and kissed him on the cheek.

- Daughter, do you know what time it is?

44

- It's half past twelve. Daddy, I'm not a little girl anymore.

- And who were you walking with?

Asya flashed with embarrassment and said uncertainly:

- With Rafik.

- Is it serious?

- Yes, Dad, it's very serious.

- My girl, are you sure of your feelings? Are you sure you'll be happy in Rafik's family? After all, we are Armenians and they are Azerbaijanis. I mean habits, traditions, customs. How will you live together? - Suren Sergeyevich looked intently into his daughter's beautiful eyes.

- Dad, I am sure that everything will be all right with me and Rafik! What traditions and customs are you talking about? We've known each other for years. We all have a Baku mentality, a common circle of acquaintances. We listen to the same music, read the same books. We have common interests!

- Maybe you're right, my daughter... Rafik is a good guy, I like him too.

After this conversation Rafik's parents, a retired military colonel and his mother, who was a housewife, came to Asya's house to ask her to marry Rafik. The guests were seated at a laid table. Suren Sergeyevich instructed that sweet tea should be served. According to the custom, the bride's parents served this drink as a sign of their consent to the engagement.

- Arif-muallim, my friend! We are fellow countrymen, you were born in Shusha, and I was born in Stepanakert. We both grew up in the graceful land of Karabakh. And now we're going to be relatives. God bless our children!

Soon they had a wonderful wedding. The young couple had a vacation on the Danube River. It was their honeymoon. It was 1987.

The newlyweds got a two-room apartment. A year later they had a beautiful daughter, named Aida. Arif-muallim was more happy about his granddaughter than anyone else. He had already retired and was able to spend a lot of time with his sweetheart. Grandpa Arif spoiled Aida as much as he could.

One evening Rafik came home from work. Asya was already home.

She came up to her husband and hugged him.

- I love you so much! - The girl whispered, resting her head against his chest.

- And I love you, my babe, replied Rafik, smiling and holding his wife close to him.

- I feel so good that I'm even scared... I feel as if I'm dreaming. And if I wake up, everything will be gone... - These strange feelings brought tears to her eyes.

- What are you saying, my love? We're fine. And it's going to be even better!

- Oh, Rafik, I don't want better... Let it be as it is now.

Do you promise?

- Of course, my dear, I promise...

1988 was a fatal year not only for Azerbaijan, but also for the entire Soviet Union. It can be considered the beginning of the end of the huge country.

Quite unexpectedly for all his relatives Suren Sergeyevich was promoted to the Moscow prosecutor's office and offered Rafik and Asya to move to the capital together with all of their family. But Rafik flatly refused to leave his native land and his relatives. It was hard for Asya to part with her parents, but she did not insist on relocation.

A year later Armen's father was reassigned to Yerevan and they moved to Armenia. That's when the connection between childhood friends was finally cut off. The first military clashes between Armenians and Azerbaijanis in the Nagorno-Karabakh Autonomous Region began.

Chapter 7

Rafik got a strict order to capture Height X at any cost. Behind it was a strategic point, accessible by the only road defended by the Armenians fortified on that height. The path was clearly visible by day and night, and there was no way to take it by storm, even with the help of large military forces. Rafik was required to destroy the enemy stronghold so that the main military units could get to the important object and capture it. Taking the target in open battle was impossible, Rafik was well aware of that. Decisive action was fraught with personnel loss and the loss of pieces of equipment. So he decided to bypass the post and hit it from the rear, counting on the unexpected attack. The maneuver required crossing a great distance.

The southern slope of the peak, from where the road was clearly visible, was bare and sloping, while its northern part remained relatively steep and covered with a hard-to-grasp forest. Closer to the peak, the vegetation gave way to dense grass, which in turn turned into bare rocks at the very peak, where the Armenian post was located to control the approaches.

Rafik planned to infiltrate the forest under the cover of night, pass through it and attack the outpost from the rear. According to preliminary calculations, this could take about ten hours of rapid marching.

At five o'clock in the morning, a mobile unit of twelve people moved along the planned route. For three hours they circled around the height and then, turning sharply to the south, began to climb the steep northern slope, getting further and further into the forest thicket. It was getting harder to hike.

Lieutenant Rafik Askerov was a brave man and had proved himself a clever and inventive commander who could be trusted with difficult operations. He always tried to save his people from useless death, so he did not act headlong, but judiciously and thoughtfully. Of course, if it was within his competence. The orders of his superiors, whatever they were, had to be followed without discussion.

This time it was Rafik who had to figure out the details of the operation. The plan he developed minimized the risk to the unit's personnel and seemed the most realistic.

In the middle of the road, the commander decided to take a break to give the soldiers ten to fifteen minutes to rest. Rafik lay down on the ground, closed his eyes, and relaxed. His thoughts immediately took him far away, to Baku... He remembered how he and Armen accompanied Volodya to Rostov-on-Don. When all the guests left, the boys were left in a room together. They hugged each other and promised never to forget each other and to do everything they could to help their friend in case one of them got into trouble. Armen left after Volodya... Then the Karabakh war began, and Rafik volunteered for the war...

Suddenly the forest music was interrupted by an automatic burst, and one of the squad members screamed in pain. He rolled to the ground and rolled to the nearest tree, caught on it, and froze motionlessly. Rafik commanded to get down on the ground and get ready to fight. The squad was attacked from three points of fire. Rafik saw his fighters throw up their arms, dropping their weapons.

Rafik's group happened to run into an Armenian unit that was on its way to the roadblock to reinforce it with manpower. The Armenians spotted the enemy first. A fierce battle ensued. The only cover they had was in the trees. The Armenians had the advantage of being at the top, while Rafik and his soldiers were at the bottom. The slope was steep, shooting back and moving back at the same time was difficult.

The battle suddenly started but ended just suddenly as well. The forest fell into silence, and for the first time, Rafik was able to look around. The corpses of the dead fighters from both sides lay all around him. After a few minutes, he cautiously peeked out from behind a tree and instantly ran over behind another. However, nothing happened. It was quiet and peaceful, with only the chirping of birds. It was the usual forest noise, to which you get used quickly and perceive it as an insignificant background. The unexpected crunch of a dry branch made Rafik tense up and fire an automatic round in the direction from which the sound came. After a minute the silence returned, and Rafik realized that whoever was hiding behind the trees twenty meters away had run out of ammunition. A white piece of cloth appeared from behind a trunk. It looked like the enemy had decided to surrender, and following the white shirt that had been used to give the signal of surrender, the man himself appeared.

Holding his assault rifle ready, Rafik cautiously looked out from behind the barrel and saw that in front of him with raised hands stood... Armen.

- You... Rafik? - he whispered and his legs went weak. Rafik stood silent, still pointing his red-hot weapon towards Armen, and couldn't make a sound either. As if they were stones, they looked at each other and did not know what to say.

A single shot tore through the silence of the forest. The bullet hit Rafik in the back of the head and he staggered to his knees and collapsed without uttering a word. It turned out that the soldier, lying not far from where the commander was standing, had woken up from his unconsciousness and fired at the enemy. Armen thought he screamed, but all that came out of his throat was a faint croak. In two jumps he found himself next to the shooter, knocked the gun out of his hands, and shot the entire clip at his friend's killer.

Throwing the gun away, Armen ran to his friend, bent over him, and carefully lifted his head. Rafik was no longer breathing. His face, contorted with pain, was marked forever by confusion and shock. Embracing the lifeless body of his friend, Armen wept bitterly.

When the first wave of grief passed and Armen regained his ability to think, he realized that he did not know what to do. But he could not leave Rafik's body lying on the ground. Looking around, the boy saw that night had completely enveloped the forest. The mountain ranges could be seen in the distance, and there was intimidating darkness of the night all around. Suddenly the image of Aunt Maryam, Rafik's mother, appeared before Armen's eyes. She was looking at him with such hope, with such entreaty in her eyes... The boy squeezed his eyes shut and shook his head, trying to get rid of the heart-burning vision.

"What should I do?" - he thought feverishly.

Finally, a decision was made. He lifted the body on his shoulders and cautiously made his way down the slope. He decided to walk in the direction of the forward units of the Azerbaijani army. At least, he thought they were there. Armen had been walking for about three hours. He was very tired and, exhausted, could hardly drag his feet. Finally, it was decided to rest. Carefully laying Rafik's body on the grass, he sat down beside him, wrapping his arms around his head. Thoughts swirled in his head...

Was Rafik's death really necessary to understand the horror people did to each other...? Why is it so hard to figure out what we live for? Five minutes ago, he was shooting at hated Azerbaijanis, and now he was sitting and crying over the body of an Azerbaijani compatriot. Human beings are monstrous angels and cruel martyrs in one person, and after what happened, he will not be able to take a gun anymore. People cry, feel compassion and love, then they kill and hate. How is it possible to combine personal aspirations with a sense of patriotism, love for the motherland, and national affiliation? How many social attitudes prevail over the poor human consciousness, how severe are the challenges that his lonely self must endure! To resist the influence from the outside, one must have an inner core, character, dignity, and principles; otherwise, all that Armen was doing now had no explanation and no meaning. Frankly speaking, at that moment he did not even think about the motives behind his actions; the feelings he had for Rafik told him what to do. It is this truth of life that is able to melt into human experience and morality, which no government, power, ideology, or bureaucrats can impose. A shared identity, affiliation with the same tribe and past unite people into a single ethnos, forming the concept of "people". A person is proud of his affiliation to this very community, he is brought up with the awareness that being someone's tribesman imposes a great responsibility on him. Such people have a high level of national dignity;

others, on the other hand, are weak in spirit and unprincipled. We are all different, and everything is too tangled up in this crazy world... But always, even in the harshest turmoil of life, we must remember that personal feelings are more important than social attitudes, especially those that divide people along national lines. This is what is called love to close people. But not to some abstract person, as Christ and his followers unsuccessfully insisted for two thousand years, but to a real flesh-and-blood person close by. This is what will really make sense to every living soul.

Guided by this personal feeling, Armen stepped toward the unknown and the danger that lay in wait for him at every turn.

Finally, a faint glimmer of light flickered ahead. It was the front line, the checkpoints of the Azerbaijani army. After an hour of walking, Armen stopped: it was not just dangerous, but reckless to go any farther.

He set Rafik's body on an open hill and made a small fire below. A breeze blew down the mountain toward the valley, carrying the smoke in the direction of the enemy's units. Giving a short shot into the starry sky, Armen broke the night silence of the mountains. It was a farewell salute in honor of an old friend. The fire was to be heard from both sides.

Hanging his weapon on his shoulder, the guy walked quickly upward and soon disappeared into the darkness. An Azerbaijani patrol, raised at the alarm, started searching the area and soon they found the body of the commander by the fire. From the outside it might have looked like Rafik was just sleeping, leaning against a tree by the cozy crackling fire, throwing off cheerful flying sparks. His documents were in his uniform pocket. The body was transported to village N, from where a military helicopter took him to Baku in a zinc coffin.

...Every day the "cargo 200" arrived in the capital of Azerbaijan. Television and newspapers reported on the fighting on a daily basis. The war was going on, blood was shed, and soldiers - husbands, sons, brothers - were killed. And the next family in Baku got a hateful death.

The city, meanwhile, lived its usual life: happy, cheerful, sad, and crying, just as before. And only meeting the next batch of the dead, they, like a red maiden, guiltily lowered the head and wished as soon as possible to survive these unpleasant but inevitable minutes, so that they could go back to their daily worries.

This half-hearted atmosphere, when there was no sense of war and no conviction of peace, and a sense of uncertainty made some Baku residents angry. It was as if the people lacked the courage and civic dignity to empathize massively with those at war - and either win or die.

Perhaps these are just big words, and when you try to put them into practice everything appears in a different light, but a small number of heroes-volunteers like Rafik never doubted for a minute that they had to defend their homeland. At the same time, their parents might have reasoned in the opposite way: why should our children die if the children of high-ranking officials and the rich are exempt from this heavy duty?

It is hard to judge these people... But this attitude to their homeland does not do honor to ordinary people, much less to the privileged classes. But there is not much we can do about it. Honor and civic dignity are either there or not. Perhaps such things are nurturing, but at the time, and even now, they are in disastrous short supply...

...Armen's father served in the military prosecutor's office in Armenia. Armen himself worked in the Ministry of Construction. The patriotic spirit of this young man was so great that he was eager to go to war as a volunteer. Contrary to his father's opinion, he enlisted as a senior lieutenant and commanded a reconnaissance platoon. For six months the boy saw all horrors of the war: blood, torments, corpses of old men, women, and children. Armen felt that something had changed in him, torn at his soul... But he could not explain it in words. All he knew was that now he could calmly look into the eyes of death.

But now he was shaking. He could not calm down. All night long he walked in bitter thoughts. Bright stars scattered across the sky illuminated his way. When it began to dawn, Armen, utterly exhausted, fell into the high intoxicating grass and lost himself in a restless sleep. When he woke up the sun was already high in the sky. The warm rays were caressing his face, trying to wake him up. It was about noon, there was a wonderful stillness all around. The birds were singing

sound of the wind, the wild beauty of Nagorno-Karabakh - all this was misleading as if there was no death nearby. The world seemed beautiful and calm. It was hard to believe that blood was being spilled here.

The decision came unexpectedly. Looking around carefully, Armen walked along a path leading to a valley with a serpentine brook at the bottom. He clearly imagined the absurdity of this endless carnage. Armenian X kills Azerbaijani Y (or vice versa) because of territory N, and it seems natural to him and all mankind. But as soon as a particular Armenian confronts a particular Rafik on the battlefield, it becomes an incomprehensible, the most monstrous nightmare. Such a situation is absurd and cannot justify existing reality! Mutually exterminating each other Armenian X and Azerbaijani Y could potentially become friends in the near future. In fact, future friends and even relatives are mutilating and destroying each other in the name of appropriating the piece of land where they already live side by side. Unthinkable!

No, Armen stubbornly told himself, what we are doing is madness! We will be cursed, all of us will be cursed, and there will be no happiness on this earth for anyone!

Descending to the river, he walked along the bank upstream, but he was stopped by a threatening shout that sounded from somewhere above:

- Freeze!...

Turning around, Armen saw the muzzle of a submachine gun aimed at him. In order to defuse the situation, he said hello in Armenian. In response, he was told to drop his weapon on the ground, raise his hands and step back ten paces. Armen complied, but could not refrain from asking a question:

- So, don't you recognize your people anymore?

- Now we'll see who's our people and who's not, said a grim voice, and another machine gun pointed in his direction.

The first soldier went up to the detainee, searched him, and, finding nothing suspicious, escorted him to a nearby village. An Armenian outpost was located there. Armen told how his unit came under fire and that he, the only survivor, hid in the forest. When asked how he ended up here, Armen was unable to give a coherent answer. After the interrogation, he was taken to a punishment cell that consisted of a wooden room with an iron door and bars on the window. The floor was riddled with a smell of rot.

For reasons of secrecy, Armen's squad was dressed in protective clothing, without distinctive military insignia or documents. They knew only the password, which was their key to all checkpoints.

A few hours later, the unit commander contacted the headquarters and received confirmation of the existence of Armen Djangirov, the squad leader. It was decided to send the detainee to the district center where the division headquarters was located in order to clarify details. Armen and two convoyers were put into the back of an old truck. It was a three-hour drive.

The car was going uphill along a serpentine road with great difficulty.

Suddenly the engine rumbled and stopped.

- What happened? - The convoyer shouted.

- Oh, the old car was smoky! We need water for the radiator.

The driver deftly picked up the bucket and went deeper into the woods in search of a water stream.

Armen and his convoy jumped down to stretch their legs, stiff from a long and motionless sitting. The senior convoyer opened the cabin door, lit a cigarette, and loudly asked Armen where he was from. When he heard that he was from Baku, he looked at his companion meaningfully, for it was known that almost all the Armenian refugees from Baku had left for Russia or other countries. Armen explained that he was not a refugee and had left the city before the sad events began.

- Tell us honestly, why did you find yourself on a completely different side of your military unit?

- I was shell-shocked after the battle, and when I recovered, I temporarily lost my bearings and was walking at random.

The convoyer looked at him doubtfully.

- There is no way out, they will squeeze the truth out of you anyway! Armen indifferently shrugged and turned away.

At that time a reconnaissance unit of Azerbaijanis found a man walking with a bucket of water. Having followed him, they saw how he slowly approached the car, opened the hood, and began to pour water into the radiator.

There was a burst of gunfire. The convoyer standing nearby collapsed to the ground, wounded by the bullets. The other convoyer, with maddened eyes, fired wildly toward the woods. A return burst of gunfire knocked him to the ground and he fell face down.

A truck door slammed. It was the driver trying to start the car. Armen reflexively turned to the back of the truck and stretched out his hand, trying to reach the side, but immediately felt a burning pain in his back and heart area. He staggered, then took a few steps forward, involuntarily threw his arms back, and, grasping the air, collapsed on his back.

The truck was shot up and burst into flames together with the driver...

Armen's body was never found. He was considered missing. His parents did not lose hope that their son had returned. They believed that Armen would one day appear on their doorstep, quietly open the door, walk up to his mother, hug and kiss her wrinkled forehead. And his mother will embrace him with a relieved heart, and her eyes will fill with tears of happiness, which will involuntarily roll down her sunken cheeks. They would sit like that for a long, long time... And then the voice of his father will be heard:

- Darling, let me hug our son, too! And they will hug each other tightly, like men.

The war... That is the time when parents outlive their children. Damn it!

Chapter 8

After leaving Rafik's mother, Joseph, shocked by everything he had heard, wandered aimlessly through the streets for an hour. Then, having come to his senses, he stopped the car and drove back to his hotel. He could not believe that his two friends were dead.

"How is it possible...? Why had this happened?" - he asked himself incessantly.

After the heat, noise, bustle, and dust of the city streets, his room felt unusually cool and quiet. Somewhere pleasant light music was playing.

Josef has taken a shower. He had no appetite. He poured himself a whiskey, collapsed heavily into a soft armchair, and stared at one point. He remained in such anabiosis for quite a long time, until the phone call brought him back to reality. A guest had been invited to a business dinner, which he graciously declined.

It was 9 p.m. on the clock, and Joseph felt that he could no longer stay in the room. Deciding to walk along the night boulevard, the young man went outside and slowly wandered along the promenade.

When he saw the sign of a night bar, a bright neon glow inviting late-night visitors, he decided to go in. On the other side of the door was a large hall, barely illuminated. Jazz was softly blasting from the ceiling. Several people were seated at the bar, and there were individual cubicles along the perimeter of the room, complete with upholstered furniture. The audience looked very respectable, and English was heard everywhere.

Joseph ordered a whiskey and soda. He was not particularly fond of alcohol, and after the third drink, he felt a little nauseous. When he was about to leave, he noticed men approaching the bar who had ordered cognac and vodka. Joseph turned his attention to the one sitting closer to him.

"Such a familiar face..." - he thought.

So many years had passed, and some formerly familiar features faded in his memory...

"Could it be Azad...?" - he suddenly realized.

The man behind the counter resembled a boy who had once lived in the house next door and sometimes came to play in their yard. Staring at him, Joseph was embarrassed: the neighbor noticed his intense attention and turned his head. Their eyes met.

- Excuse me, but you remind me of someone... - Joseph said.

- You know, your face looks familiar to me, too. But I can't tell you where I've seen you before," the man replied.

- You look like an old friend of mine named Azad, Joseph revealed.

- That's right, I am Azad, the man said, still trying to guess who he was talking to.

- Azad! I am Joseph from next door!

- The same Joseph who used to go to Israel? - he exclaimed.

- Well, yes, that's right. Except that I live in the United States.

- Oh, it's good to see you! - Azad got up from his chair and approached the old acquaintance. They embraced warmly.

- Joseph, can we speak on a first-name basis? The man nodded his head.

- Look, I wouldn't even recognize you! You have changed and you look so respectable. A hundred percent American!

- No way! I'm still the same Joseph. And how are you doing?

- I have... Oh, excuse me... This is my friend Oktay.

- Nice to meet you, Joseph shook Oktay's hand.

- As for me, I am a professor, I lecture in history and political science at the university, - said Azad. - Joseph, I'm sorry, but I see that you do not feel comfortable... Is something wrong?

- Two days ago I came here on a business trip for the company I work for. And today I went to visit Aunt Maryam. Do you remember Rafik's mother?

- Yes, of course. So you already know about it? - The man asked with a change of face.

- It's horrible! I still can't believe that the boys are dead.

- I went to Rafik's funeral. You know what... Let's order a drink!

We'll sit in the cubicle, nobody will bother us, and we'll talk.

They sat down in comfortable armchairs and talked about their childhood, but Joseph couldn't concentrate. Thoughts of his fallen friends kept running through his mind.

- Listen, Azad, I left here as a teenager. The American newspapers at the time were reporting on the Karabakh conflict, but always from the Armenian point of view. Now I realize that I didn't know the Azerbaijani side at all.

- Joseph, when we talk about national conflicts, which can include the Karabakh conflict, first of all we must keep in mind that there are several objective reasons for this strife. We can say that at that time everything came together at one point.

As you know, the world is ruled by power, i.e. force. It is either too much or not enough, but it is always there. At the end of the eighties, power in the Soviet Union weakened. And a totalitarian state can only live by the principle of communicating vessels: if power weakens in the center, it flows to the periphery. Feeling a sense of relief, the nationalists raised their heads - in this case, it was in the form of separatism - and managed to infect their countrymen with a heightened sense of pseudo-nationalism of sickly adolescent nature. The center tried to control such outbursts, use them to its advantage, and write political scenarios. But at the time, there was a fight for power in the center itself. And the processes on the ground began to deepen and take on an autonomous character, even though they ran within the framework of the schemes that were established from above. That's the first thing. And second, as a result of all this in real life - not in schemes and plans - blood was shed, people suffered the loss of their own land and native homes, the death of loved ones, resentment, and hate. Once again, all of this was the result of cunning political schemes, and theories disconnected from reality. The most terrible thing here is human grief, and let historians and political scientists work out the circumstances and reasons. Judgments of average citizens are well reflected by a widespread phrase: "Gorbachev is to blame for everything! He ruined such a country!" And no one explains what kind of "such a country" it is. They say it is well-known.

- Why were the Azerbaijanis silent? Why, like the Armenians, did not stand up for their truth, did not trumpet their own version of events to the world? - Joseph reasonably remarked.

- You are looking at the root! Azerbaijanis have always lacked talented representatives, who could bring their truth to the West. I think -perhaps I am wrong, -the problems of information disunity also lie in the fact that Azerbaijanis are perceived as part of the Islamic world. In fact, they are. But in 1988 even the population of Azerbaijan itself did not think so.

- I remember well our atheistic life, - said Joseph thoughtfully.

- So, Azerbaijan itself and information coming from the republic were perceived by the West through the prism of stereotypes about the Islamic world. Consequently, the Western public a priori received a distorted picture of our state. Not to mention the fact that any voice, even the babbling of children, sounded in defense of the Azerbaijanis, the republic's authorities tried to muffle or twist it so that Moscow liked it.

The Armenians, in turn, as representatives of the Christian world, had very powerful guides, whose weighty voices were understood in the West. And this is without taking into account how thoroughly and extensively Armenian nationalists and separatists were prepared for this conflict with the help of the Armenian world community. On our side, the stupidity, self-interest, and fear of the Azerbaijani authorities, the inability to govern their own people, and the weakness of spirit of the majority of the population have led to the situation in which we are now. You see, the honor and dignity of Azerbaijanis have been dealt a tangible blow. And we still can't recover from it. That's what should be understood and remembered before analyzing the conflict that took place in detail, Azad concluded his long monologue.

Then he raised his glass in thought:

- Let us once again drink to Rafik and Armen, so that their souls may meet in the other world and continue their friendship, interrupted by human madness! Truly, Christ said, people do not realize what they do.

- Azad, Russian-language newspapers in America always referred to the Baku and Sumgait massacres against Armenians as cruel and inhumane in their publications on the Karabakh conflict. Was it really impossible to do without such extreme measures? I cannot even believe that Azerbaijanis are capable of what was reported.

Moscow and the scriptwriters of this conflict were well aware that it would not be easy to take away Karabakh and give it to the Armenians. It had to make it smart. But Moscow could not come up with anything smarter than war. And war became inevitable.

- When the confrontation between Azerbaijan and Armenia turned into a hot phase, Armenians in Azerbaijan and Azerbaijanis in Armenia turned into hostages. Imagine the bodies of dead soldiers arriving in Baku and Yerevan. What must the relatives of these unfortunates feel, and how must they restrain themselves from the temptation to avenge them? And this revenge was a heavy burden on the shoulders of the closest neighbors.

The Azerbaijanis were dealt with very harshly. In January 1989 more than 230,000 of these people were expelled from their homes in Armenia. Unlike their Armenian brothers in misfortune, the Azerbaijani refugees were forced to leave absolutely everything - houses, property, livestock, and travel on foot to the borders of the country. Since their exile was not spontaneous but organized, it was carried out within two weeks. Children, women, and the elderly walked across snow-covered mountain passes. No one counted those who froze on the way. The then First Secretary of the Azerbaijani Central Committee, Vezirov, did not allow the Azerbaijani refugees from Armenia to remain in the Nagorno-Karabakh Autonomous Region, whose population at the time was 180,000 - 140,000 Armenians and 40,000 Azerbaijanis. If another 230,000 Azerbaijanis had settled there, I think things could have gone differently. That's why all the refugees - the entire rural population of Armenia - were sent to Baku and Sumgait.

Another proof that Moscow has already decided to give Karabakh to the Armenians.

Can you imagine, people expelled from Armenia were allowed into cities where hundreds of thousands of Armenians lived? The authorities only had to throw a burning match into this gasoline tank, which they did not fail to do. By the way, the ringleader of the criminals operating in Sumgayit was a three-time jailed local Armenian. That's it.

- Where were the police, the army? - Joseph interrupted him.

- The army? That's a good question. Look, the massacres in Baku lasted from January 13 to 19, 1990. Armenians were rescued from criminals by ordinary Azerbaijani citizens, neighbors, and acquaintances. And the authorities simply organized the evacuation of refugees - by a ferry running between Baku and Krasnovodsk. Not a single Soviet Army soldier left his barracks located directly in the city to set order. There were simply no orders.

- Azad, I realized only now that I didn't even ask Maryam-khanum where Rafik was buried...

- Do you remember Kirov Park?

- Of course, I do.

- Well, the upper part of the Nahorny Park, as it's called now, was turned into the Alley of Honourable Burial. There our soldiers who died in Karabakh were buried. Rafik's body is also buried there. If you have time, call me tomorrow at this number. - Azad held out his business card. - We will go and visit his grave.

It had been a long time since Joseph had drunk or smoked so much. He didn't get to bed until three o'clock in the morning, and barely touched the pillow he fell asleep. The phone was ringing off the hook when the man struggled to open his eyes and look at his watch.

The hands showed 10:00 in the morning. He had to be in the office by nine o'clock. Joseph struggled to get up, but a severe headache brought him back to bed.

Clutching his head, he groaned softly, remembering last night.

The phone kept ringing, and he had no choice but to answer it. The call came, of course, from the office. The voice was full of dissatisfaction. Joseph apologized and promised to be there in half an hour. A cold shower and hot, strong coffee quickly brought him to his senses. Excluding the dark circles under his eyes and the annoying noise in his head, he was almost fine.

Around 4 p.m., relieved of his duties, Joseph called Azad. They arranged to meet in front of the main entrance of Nagorny Park.

There was a tall stone stele at the foot of which an eternal flame burned. To the left of the entrance was a minaret in the Turkish style. Initially the park was named after a colleague of Joseph Stalin and the first secretary of the Leningrad Regional Committee and City Party Committee, Sergey Mironovich Kirov. He was shot under unclear circumstances before the elections to the position of General Secretary of the CPSU Central Committee, where he was preparing to compete with Stalin.

During the Soviet era, this place was one of the most popular resting places, where Baku residents of all nations and ages loved to relax. Children and teenagers were attracted by the numerous amusements, couples in love huddled together on the cozy benches set up in a secluded place, and the elderly came to communicate and breathe the fresh air. The park was literally buried in greenery. The massive tall trees, exotic plants, and a variety of flowers gave off fragrant air.

The famous "Druzhba" restaurant was also located here, offering a panoramic view of the capital. Baku in the evening was a stunning sight, spread out at the foot of the park like a luminous ocean. Families, friends, and guests from other cities and countries loved to come to this place. Above the restaurant there was a special observation deck, from which one could watch the Seaside Boulevard, a curved four-kilometer long arched coastal strip edging the Baku Bay from the top of the bird's-eye view. A huge monument to revolutionary Kirov stood in the center of the observation deck. It was demolished in 1990.

Another local attraction was the funicular, a railroad running from the foot to the top of the sea terrace, with access to the observation deck. People, especially children, filled the beautiful, brightly colored open-air cars and enjoyed the fascinating ride. After the beginning of hostilities in Nagorno-Karabakh, they decided to bury the people who died in the war in Kirov Park. So the place gradually turned into a memorial cemetery, and at its entrance flamed eternal flame in memory of fallen sons of the motherland. In just a few months thousands and thousands of graves filled the upper part of the park.

Azad was the first to arrive at the meeting place. He found an empty bench, sat down and lit a cigarette. His thoughts ran as fast as they could, stirring up images of his childhood, youth and student years.

- I'm sorry I'm a little late, Azad, he heard Joseph's voice and held out his hand. - The traffic is so heavy, you can't get through quickly.

Completely immersed in his own thoughts, the professor did not immediately realize what he was being told.

- It's all right, Joseph, it's all right, let's go.

They entered the park, followed the shady alley, and soon an astonished view opened to his guest, which shook him to his core. Countless tombstones of the same kind were rising in rows beyond the horizon and disappearing into the distance.

- How many were there...? - Joseph whispered in shock.

All the graves were numbered. Rafik's grave was numbered 1856. His portrait had been engraved on the marble tombstone. A handsome, strong-willed face looked with some sadness in his gaze. Joseph laid a large bouquet of scarlet roses.

The men stood in silence for a while and smoked a cigarette. Then they slowly walked back. At the exit, Joseph turned around and cast a goodbye glance at the cemetery.

Azad told him that the first to be buried in the park were the victims of Black January. Grave number one belonged to a young couple who had been married the day before. Grave number two was the grave of a twelve-year-old girl.

- After the Armenian massacres and the Armenian exodus from Baku was largely completed, on the night of 19 to 20 January 1990 the Soviet Army entered the city.

- What did this invasion have to do with the massacres? - Joseph asked.

As you understand, the purpose of the invasion of the military in Baku was not at all the salvation of the Armenians. The pogroms, diligently orchestrated. And staged by the USSA State Security Committee (KGB) , had already been stopped by that moment

- It is not difficult to understand that the main purpose of the entry of troops into Baku was not at all to save Armenians. The authorities wanted to prevent the elections to the Supreme Soviet of Azerbaijan, scheduled for February 1990, from taking place as in any normal country. It was clear that the victory of supporters of Azerbaijani independence was predetermined and the central authorities did not want to accept it. The Lithuanian version of events in our republic was prevented by punitive action. The operation under the codename " Strike" involved 20,000 servicemen of the Soviet Army and internal troops. Under the slogans of establishing constitutional order, the Soviet Union government launched a massacre on January 20, 1990, to prevent Azerbaijan's secession from the USSR. Unarmed citizens went to the streets and built barricades, protesting against the introduction of military forces in Baku. But how could they resist such a force?

Soviet tanks passed through the whole city Baku, crushing and shooting peaceful Soviet citizens, old people, women and children on their way.

In the end, they even shot an ambulance, killing the doctor and the driver. By the way, maybe you used to know this man. The doctor's name was Boris Reznik. He was a good guy... All those who were killed that awful night was buried in Kirov Park. Listen, Joseph, you're leaving tomorrow... Let's sit down, talk, have lunch. When will we see each other again?

So they did. Azad took Joseph to the countryside, to a restaurant in the forest. Elegant tables with comfortable soft chairs, neatly paved walkways, and beautiful lanterns in the Art Nouveau style created a cozy atmosphere. Courteous waiters with trays handed out delicious dishes, not making visitors wait long.

They sat down at a suggested place, and Joseph and Azad ordered drinks, snacks, and kebabs.

- How things have changed here! - remarked the American visitor once again. - I have a double feeling... On the one hand, everything is familiar, and on the other, everything is new and unfamiliar.

- Yes, Joseph, during these eighteen years everything has happened on this land... It's a small period of time by historical standards, but how much has happened! People haven't even had time to realize it yet.

- Assad, what do you think needs to be done to restore relations between Azerbaijan and Armenia? It cannot last forever...

- Why not? Conflicts of this kind can last for decades. I think the problem of our compatriots lies elsewhere. Azerbaijanis have to sort themselves out before they do anything. Otherwise... you see for yourself what kind of trouble we've made in the years of your absence.

I believe the misfortune of our people, as well as some others, is that they have lived to this day without becoming a united nation with the proper level of national consciousness. It is easy for all those intellectuals and liberals in civilized Western countries to condemn nationalism and preach globalization, universal human brotherhood, and peace without borders. Western nations have passed through this necessary stage of development, which reached its peak with the Fascist revolts. It was a developed sense of national dignity that helped these nations get where they are today.

Joseph was quite distant from the subject Azad had touched upon, so he struggled to understand what he was saying.

Meanwhile, the professor continued:

- When one nation is figuring things out with another, there is little dependence on the personal dignity of each individual citizen. In this case, we should speak of a high level of national, i.e., collective dignity. The same man can fight back against the offender of his wife and at the same time refrain from defending his insulted homeland.

It costs the civilized nations of the West nothing to make wishes and recommendations to other nations to forsake inter-ethnic strife and live amicably as in a united Europe. They are now living with post-nationalist ideas and are busy forming various political, financial, and economic alliances. Really, it is ridiculous of them to demand from the countries of the former Soviet Union and the Third World to urgently skip the stage of the formation of national consciousness! Ethnic dignity grows only on the basis of good nationalism. And all problems lie not in the fact that someone seeks power or encroaches on someone else's territory, but in the collective pride and self-assertion. This is the real source of wars, global and local, this is the driving force behind the seizure of territorial space belonging to a neighbor!

- Azad, I do not understand the connection between national dignity and international conflicts.

- The connection is because national dignity is so burdened by all kinds of human vices and virtues that it cannot be discerned at a glance. It is difficult to grasp at once the pivotal importance of national self-consciousness in people's history. For example, what does it mean to offend a human being? First of all, it means degrading a human being's dignity. And what does it mean to take away a person's freedom? To humiliate his civil dignity. It is the same with an entire people. It can be humiliated, insulted, or dishonored, and if a nation has a low level of national consciousness, it will tolerate, it will lose, because it cannot and will not want to defend itself. An ethnos with high national dignity, on the contrary, will win and yearn for new achievements, because it believes it is worthy.

- You have an original way of looking at things! Especially when we are witnessing an obvious outburst of nationalism around the world.

- Exactly! Civilized countries, which have entered the phase of post-nationalism, are unhappy with the outburst of national tensions in backward countries. As luck would have it, this conflict coincided with the advent of post-industrialism and the development of the information society, when the world was reduced to the size of a glowing little blue screen. Globalization has done its work, and any inter-ethnic strife, even a minor one, becomes public and is fraught with profound consequences. Nothing can be done about it, as the development of national consciousness cannot be restrained. That is why Western countries feel uncomfortable and insecure in this world. You have to agree that they have something to lose besides their national pride.

- So it turns out that even technological progress is driven by the development of nationalism?

- Of course, it is! Isn't the connection between nationalism and economic success obvious? There is a direct correlation. The brighter the national consciousness, the greater its economic success. I do not think that national dignity is simply the sum of the personal advantages of individuals of the same ethnicity. That would be too simple. As an example, you can take any economically developed country, whose nationalism is more solidified and qualitative than Azerbaijan's. Nationalism is the base on which all other differences of an ethnos are superimposed. So every nation, if it really wants to achieve something, must go through a phase of nationalism, like getting over chicken pox in childhood. It is not chauvinism, fascism, communism, or religion; it is merely a natural sense of dignity.

- Well, these thoughts have merit. But what to do if it is poorly expressed? What should we even do now, given the realities of modern life?

- I think national dignity grows gradually; it may take decades. It is not just a love for the homeland, for the land where a person was born and lives, because these feelings are inherent in all nations without any exceptions. National consciousness, rather, determines the maturity of a nation, its cohesion, historical responsibility, and, eventually, the willingness to sacrifice on a conscious level, not on the affective one. After all, for the sake of a high level of self-consciousness, people must dare to leave their comfort zone, to sacrifice their usual way of life and sometimes their own lives and the destinies of their loved ones. Emotions and feelings are powerless here, because they reflect a desire to remain at the mercy of the body, instincts, and the craving for pleasure. Unfortunately, we are in a time crunch.

- So what are the Azerbaijani authorities doing to somehow alleviate the plight of hundreds of thousands of refugees from the occupied lands? Is it helping them to return to their homes?

Unsurprised by Joseph's naivety, Azad shrugged his shoulders:

- Are you asking me about power? In their actions, these structures go as far as the people allow. Look, the spirit of Azerbaijan is broken now, the people have accepted the situation. If a single person loses his dignity - that's half the trouble. But when the majority loses it, it's a real catastrophe! People are beginning to live one day at a time, just as our government has been doing for years. They are not a full-fledged government, but temporary workers who see their immediate goal as getting the biggest piece of the national wealth. It is frightening that the people themselves become temporaries in their own country! People do not think or do not want to think about their children, who are the future. And this is already schizophrenic...

- Azad, what is the current situation with the army?

- I am not competent enough in this matter. But if you make conclusions on the basis of media data, there are a lot of problems in our troops. I think they are not ready for war. Moreover, I emphasize that we need well-developed power structures not for attacking, but to strengthen our authority at the negotiating table. What is the point of other states having a conversation as equals with a country that can't stand up for itself?

- Azad, I'm not entirely impressed by your pessimism. If this is the way an intellectual elite thinks, what's left for the common people?

- The people, our poor people... We've just talked so much about national dignity and external influence. But there's another contagion that keeps us from living our lives to the fullest. And that is--you'll laugh--corruption!

Joseph actually smiled and threw up his hands:

- Well, it's a disease of all mankind...

- Yes, you're right. We can hardly name a single human vice that is completely absent in any ethnic group. All of us, humans, are alike. We have the same social and moral ailments. And this has long been known. But that's not what I'm talking about here. I'm talking about the measure. Every thing has its measure. Don't you agree?

- Yes, he nodded.

- If people have enough national dignity and funds, that's a good thing! But if all social structures are entangled in corruption - that's bad. Right?

- Of course, it is obvious.

- In today's Azerbaijani society, corruption has pierced all verticals of power. It has overcome the most inconceivable barriers. In the past, it was modestly known as bribery and was used when necessary. Now it has become a vital necessity, like waking up in the morning and going to the bathroom. Something like that. Corruption is everywhere: they ask for money, they give it, and sometimes they shove it by force or harass them with threats. Two generations of doctors have grown up on bribes! And now it is clear that most of our population is being treated by incompetent doctors who have bought their diplomas. As an American, can you imagine the threat to our nation's physical health? A corrupt network, like an octopus, has entwined Azerbaijan's universities and descended even into the secondary level of education, the schools. Who teaches our children? Teachers who got their diplomas for bribes. How do they teach them? The answer is- bribes. This is ethnic castration in its purest form!

Mortified by what he had heard, Joseph had nothing to say to his old friend and only shook his head slowly. He was horrified by what he had heard.

- What do you think determined the collapse of the Soviet Union?
- Finally, he decided to break the painful silence.

- It's difficult to say unequivocally, said Azad. - There are many reasons, both external and internal. One is the events in Poland that shook the Warsaw Pact camp to its foundations. Then the Afghan war began the wound that had erupted in the body of the Soviet empire. At that time, the price of oil went down to $14 to $15 a barrel. Then came Reaganomics, with its arms race, the Strategic Defense Initiative announced by Reagan, and so forth.

But the most important internal factor was the coming to power of Gorbachev and his team, as well as the miserable economic situation in the country. After them, Yeltsin put all the "dots over and", and abolished the Soviet Union. We all have yet to contemplate the Great Decade that shook the world. In this case, I mean the period from 1986 to 1996.

In my opinion, the most fateful and mysterious of these events was that they all converged on Azerbaijan, or rather, on Nagorno-Karabakh, which was the detonator, the beginning of the end of the Soviet Empire, of the Soviets. A small autonomous region turned into the epicenter of the world cataclysms of the late twentieth century!

Remember, usually, a strong earthquake is preceded by minor tremors which are a kind of warning about the impending disaster. The riots in Alma-Ata, followed by aftershocks in Georgia, Fergana, Tajikistan, Chechnya, and Moldova were a test case. When trouble comes, open the gates: the conflicts in Yugoslavia and Albania were not long in coming. The empire was engulfed by a ring of fire and death took control. The bony old woman did her best to taunt the common people. The smell of blood and the sense of death sharpened the basest instincts. Absolute evil triumphed, and all the good intentions, if any part of the people had them, turned into a double disaster, an even greater tragedy! In a short period of time, holy, beautiful ideas and selfless, honest, ideological deeds were discredited. All the deeds of mankind were drowned in the stench of decay and mother's tears...

- You know, Azad, I look at the collapse of the Soviet Union a little differently. Taking into account the grandiose scale of the event, which, naturally, couldn't do without victims and suffering, everything happened relatively peacefully and was done with little blood. Compare: over the millennia, many empires disappeared from the planet, killing hundreds of thousands of people. In the twentieth century, people experienced terrible wars and revolutions that took perhaps hundreds of millions of lives. And the Soviet regime itself destroyed tens of millions of citizens during its brief century. Compared to that nightmare, the downfall of the Soviet colossus was relatively peaceful.

- I agree that this is not comparable in scale. Except that deaths always remain deaths, no matter how many there are. Needless to say, the very fact of the collapse of the seemingly indestructible empire, the fall of the Berlin Wall, and the debunking of the Communist myth - all this shocked and disoriented contemporaries. In the terrible times of the Great Patriotic War, at least it was clear: here was the enemy, he attacked us, and everyone has the same goal - to protect the wounded homeland. After the events of the early 1990s, there is still chaos in people's minds. Something incomprehensible has happened, something that defies interpretation. And all the anger, all the curses fell on one man - Mikhail Gorbachev. He was destined to become the main scapegoat. He is the one who is still cursed by the former citizens of the now-defunct country.

- By the way, our emigrants in America agree with them. They also believe that Gorbachev is the main culprit for their departure and claim that he ruined the beautiful country where you could travel anywhere you wanted for forty to fifty rubles, where money was money, and life was real life. Can you imagine that, Azad? Oh, no, you can't imagine how unfair people can be! - Joseph finished indignantly.

Azad only smiled and nodded.

- Look, - after a short pause Joseph continued, - what do you think about the religious renaissance in the world and in Azerbaijan in particular? I noticed that people are seriously thinking about faith and God. At least this is unexpected because we all grew up in an atmosphere of harsh antireligious propaganda.

- Yes, you're right. People are starting to go back to their roots, from which they were once torn. As for me, you know that I was born into Islam. But my personal sympathies are on the side of Protestant ethics. I am not an advocate of religious rituals and formal worship. Rather, I intuitively believe in a supreme being, the Creator, and seek to feel him in me without any assistance or words. I consider religious structures to be an extension of political, economic, and social instances, which are created in the interests of certain groups in order to control people in the name of God. They control minds-and, alas, not without success; they try to dominate souls. As for me, I think that everyone should measure his/her words and deeds with the thought that God sees and hears everything. I believe that God is one and indivisible, and I imagine him as a certain perfect being who is the main architect of the universe. I am convinced that any religious dissent is alien to his will.

Joseph said goodbye to Azad and passed him an envelope:

- There is money in it. Please give it to Aunt Maryam, Rafik's mother. Here are the address and phone number.

- Don't worry, I'll take care of it.

- I don't know if we'll see each other again... And they hugged each other tightly.

Despite the late hour, Joseph went to his old courtyard again, hoping to see Aunt Dusya. This time he was greeted by a small, hunched-over, dried out old woman. Only in her squinting eyes did she still shine with life and curiosity. Even eighteen years ago she had seemed very old to Joseph, and now she was also hard of hearing, so Joseph had to almost shout to explain everything. Joseph learned from her that Volodya and his mother moved to Rostov-on-Don, and he got the address, because Aunt Dusya initially carried on a little correspondence with Volodya's mother. Then the connection was cut off, and now there was no news.

Joseph was determined to find his childhood friend. After everything he had experienced in Baku, he just needed to meet a close person and relieve his soul.

Chapter 9

The next morning, having completed his duties, Joseph flew from Baku to Rostov-on-Don, and at 2 p.m. he was already stepping off the plane.

It was as if he were in the past. The provincial airport building had not changed much since Soviet times. There was the same filth, the same petty, but an intrusive inconvenience, which made the life of a traveler unbearable. Some suspicious individuals scurried back and forth, curiously examining the well-dressed and clearly different person from those around him. Joseph felt uncomfortable here. He put his suitcase in the luggage room and stopped in indecision, not knowing where to go.

A middle-aged man called out to him, which made him shudder. For a modest price, he was offered a ride into the city.

- Where are you from? - The driver asked, sensing that the man was not spatially oriented.

- From Moscow.

- Are you here on business, or with a check-up?

- No, I want to visit a friend.

- From Moscow... To visit a friend? - the chauffeur asked incredulously.

- Well, yes, we have not seen each other for a long time.

- That is a good thing! Friendship should not be forgotten.

The place that was listed in the address was far from the city center. It was a green street with two- and three-story old buildings.

Joseph generously paid the chauffeur, who thanked him until the man disappeared into the entryway. It was dark and smelled damp. After climbing a few steps, Joseph found himself on a stairway with two doors without numbers.

- Which one? - he whispered and knocked at random. There was no doorbell, either.

The door was opened by an elderly woman, and, squinting her eyes in the dark, she asked:

- Who do you need?

- Excuse me, but I'm trying to find Valentina Ivanovna Kovalyova.

- Kovalyova...? Who are you?

- I'm a childhood friend of her son, Vladimir. We lived in the same courtyard in Baku. I came from far away to see them.

- Where did you come from?

- From America.

The old woman's squinting eyes rounded momentarily, and she decided to open the door wider.

- Valya left... - she said, stopping herself.

- She left? Where? With Vladimir?

Then the old woman opened the door completely. Her tense face somehow softened.

- What is your name, dear? - she suddenly asked.

- Joseph.

- Joseph, she repeated like an echo. - It's a beautiful name, - she added for some reason. - And I am Pelageya Nikolaevna. Come inside, son, if you want. You must be tired after the trip... I'll tell you something. Once in the apartment, Joseph immediately smelled old, stale things. Usually, it smells like that in the apartments of elderly and lonely people.

Pelageya Nikolaevna guided him to the kitchen, invited him to the table, put a fresh tablecloth on it, put a sugar bowl and jam, cut a piece of cake, and made tea. Then, sitting across from Joseph, who was waiting patiently for the conversation to begin, she asked:

- Joseph, tell me, how is life there, in America?

- It depends, Pelageya Nikolaevna.

- Are people happy with their lives or not? - she insisted.

- Some are happy, others are not, the guest again answered evasively.

- It's the same here... Some people are satisfied and even very satisfied, while others swear at the authorities. Life for us, the old people, was not happy under all the Secretaries, and it still is. We have seen nothing but work, and we live out our old age in poverty. That's the way it is. Yes, it seems to be the same everywhere on earth, Pelageya Nikolayevna comforted herself.

Joseph did not change her mind.

- So what did you want to tell me? - he decided to remind her of the purpose of his visit.

- Oh, yes, I'm old now, I always forget... Valya left three years ago to stay with her younger sister in Novosibirsk. Her older sister Maria died here five years ago.

After a pause, she continued thoughtfully:

- Yes, I remember Volodya... He was a good guy. So polite, so nice. He loved his mother very much. All neighbors respected him. People at work respected him, too.

Joseph couldn't take it anymore and decided to interrupt her:

- Why do you speak in the past tense? Why he was a good guy?

The old woman, downcast her eyes, cleared her throat:

- He's not alive now... He died in Chechnya...

At that moment Joseph, who had never expected such a turn of events, began to rise slowly from his chair. His face turned white as a ghost, and his fists clenched in powerless anger.

The old woman, quite frightened, jumped up to him and, putting her arm around his shoulders, wept:

- Sonny! Darling! Are you alright? Sit down on the couch, son, come on, that's ok, sit down, dear! - She gently pulled him down, sat him down on the couch, and ran to the kitchen to get some water.

Joseph sat down, dropped his head on his knees, put his hands around his face, and wept bitterly.

The old woman even gasped in shock. She had not seen an intelligent, well-dressed, and sober man cry for a long time, so she was completely confused. Then she walked over and began stroking his beautiful, curly light brown hair.

With this unknown woman, Joseph felt completely free, as if he were alone. Even in front of his parents, he would have been ashamed to show such intense emotion. But now, completely unconcerned about what it looked like from the outside, Joseph cried as he had not cried in all these eighteen years.

After a while, he fell silent, feeling as if a stone had been removed from his heart. The tears relieved his traumatized soul, which had been so unexpectedly confronted with the death of loved ones. Sobbing occasionally, he did not understand how he, always so restrained, had managed to lose his temper so much. It was as if he was mourning not only the death of his only true friends but most of his emigrant life. All the tensions that had accumulated over the years seemed to fade away. He was overwhelmed by a whole new emotion he had never experienced before.

As he regained the ability to speak, Joseph asked as if into the void:

- What happened to me?

- It's all right, it's all right, the old woman said, also feeling slightly uncomfortable and continuing to stroke the guest's head and back.

- Please excuse me... for my condition...

- What are you talking about, boy? What are you talking about? I'm so glad you came to visit me. I've been alone all day. At least I got to talk to a human being!

She took him to the bathroom and brought him a clean towel. Joseph washed his face and sat down at the table again. In the meantime, Pelageya Nikolayevna served freshly brewed tea.

- Joseph, help yourself, have a hot drink, try the cherry jam. I made it myself. I bet there's no such jam in your America. You'll see, you'll feel better! - she wouldn't stop talking.

- Yes, Pelageya Nikolaevna, they don't sell jam as good as yours there.

- Well, enjoy it, dear.

Joseph stayed with Pelageya Nikolaevna for about an hour. Before he left, he suddenly asked:

- Pelageya Nikolaevna, do you have a church nearby?

- Of course. You want to light a candle for the soul of Volodya, who was killed? That's right, son, it's a godly thing to do. Have you baptized yourself?

- Me? - Joseph hesitated.

- Oh, I was just asking... - the landlady was embarrassed. - Everything was backwards and forwards before... And now we have a good priest. Father Georgy. He is a real hearty man - he listens and calms you down, and gives advice. God bless him! Well, you'll get to know him soon enough. By the way, even I, a silly woman, have noticed that he is a very wise man. He should have a parish in Moscow, not here in the middle of nowhere, she finished.

The church Joseph went to was founded in the nineteenth century. With the establishment of Soviet power, it was closed and turned into a hardware storehouse. First, all the church property was confiscated, and then one winter day, when there was a blistering frost, several wagons drove up to the old building. The attendants gathered the clergy together and, without further explanation, took them all away to an unknown destination. The revival of the church began after "perestroika", and since then, daily worship has been conducted according to the full rules of the orthodox church.

Perfect cleanliness reigned inside. It was obvious that the temple was meticulously maintained and cared for. Almost no one was present, except a few old women praying in front of the altar.

Joseph went to the church worker and bought three candles. Then he went to the eve, set them in special slots, and lit them. He did not know what to do next, so he looked around in confusion until he heard a low yet soft man's voice behind him greeting him:

- I am glad to see a new parishioner in our humble cloister!

He turned around and saw the priest in front of him. He was a middle-aged man in a black cassock with a short beard. He had a typical Slavic broad face with protruding cheekbones, barely slanting, and deeply set blue eyes. Stroking his beard, the priest looked at the stranger inquisitively.

- Good afternoon

- I am Father Georgy, the priest of this church. Father Georgy is Peter Sergeyevich Tverskoi.

- Pleased to meet you, Father Georgy. My name is Joseph.

- Oh, it's a famous Old Testament name. And how much sense it makes to a man of faith.

- I'm flattered by such high praise. I hadn't thought of it myself before.

- You, Joseph, don't look like someone from here...

- Yes, I'm traveling here, and I'm leaving for Moscow soon.

- Where are you from?

- I live in America.

- Yes, indeed, you're from far away. And what are you doing here? If it's no secret...

- I came to visit my childhood friend. Yeah, I guess it was not meant to be...

- Joseph paused halfway through the sentence.

- Forgive me if I bother you, - said the priest, seeing how Joseph's face changed, - did something happen to you?

- Yes, Father Georgy, an old friend of mine died.

- Oh God, rest his soul! - The priest crossed himself. - How did it happen?

- Chechnya, Joseph answered briefly.

- You know what, young man... You have come from far away, and if you have some free time, I invite you to share a modest meal with me.

Joseph had booked a ticket to Moscow, the flight was scheduled for eight o'clock in the evening, so he had a few hours to spare.

- Let me ask you, have you ever visited an Orthodox church before? - Father Georgy asked.

- This is my first time in a Russian church, - Joseph answered confusedly.

Then the priest decided to give the visitor a little excursion. He explained that the church, like many other temples, has the shape of a cross at the base, for by the Cross the Savior saved people from the power of the devil. The temple building is crowned by a dome representing the sky.

On the dome, there is a head on which there is a cross to the glory of Jesus Christ. Above the entrance of the temple, there is a bell tower on which bells are hung and used for calling the congregation to prayer and announcing the most important parts of the church service.

According to the tradition the interior arrangement of the church was three-part: it consisted of the altar, the middle temple, where believers usually stood, and the vestibule. The vestibule was the place where Joseph had visited earlier. Here candles were sold, and it was possible to submit notes for remembrance and to order a prayer service or a memorial service.

Then the priest and his guest walked behind the altar and deepened to the back of the church, where the church services were located. Father Georgy approached the low, massive wooden door and, opening it, invited Joseph inside.

The young man found himself in a spacious, well-lit square room. In the middle was a long table covered with a white tablecloth. On it was snacks and food, a jug of red wine, and a single cutlery. The clergyman went to the sideboard, took out another plate, and placed it on the table, inviting Joseph to sit down.

Then the clergyman said the pre-dinner prayer, and they began to eat. The priest poured wine into glasses, and they drank to the repose of Vladimir's soul.

- May he rest in peace, God rest in peace! - Father Georgy concluded and after a short pause asked: - How do you like it here?

- I do not know, - embarrassed the guest. - Everything seems familiar... and at the same time strange, new. I haven't figured out my own feelings yet... I left this country when I was only fourteen, now I am thirty-three years old, and I have not heard anything good from anyone so far. I've lost three close friends that were in my mind all my emigrant life. And they are gone... gone! You see, I existed these eighteen years as if in another world... There, everything is different: quiet, peaceful, calm. Here there was a kind of madness... - he tried to explain in a confused way.

- I understand you, Joseph. We really had and still have terrible things going on here. The people of the new wave tore down the communist system but offered the people nothing in return. And then these orphaned souls thought of the Lord God, our Orthodox Church. But the problem is that democratic Russia is still led by party bureaucrats, specialists in scientific communism, and militant atheism. Everything is being done in Russia so that morality is free, and the soul has atrophied for lack of use. Who will be able to fix this? Society is corrupted and demoralized. Tens of millions of people are outraged but have no strength or desire to protest. Where is the power to raise...

- Sorry to interrupt you, Father Georgy, but people have indeed begun to return to the fold of the church, and even the top government officials are visiting churches...

- Yes, the religious feelings of ordinary people have awakened, and I believe that most of them are sincere. Except for the bosses, everything is mostly for show. Just a tribute to fashion! I do not think that these high-ranking officials starting with the President, congressmen and government have awakened from the darkness and are moving toward the light of God. Unfortunately, it is often just a farce.

The soul is not discussed anywhere in Russia. There are debates about whether religion should be taught at school. Of course, it is, but who is going to teach the soul?! Two times two is four, even a scoundrel can teach that. But he cannot nurture, except in a worse way. Who can be these spiritual teachers? The devotees? There are none! Hypocrites? Sorry, but better not. Will God intervene, will He want to save us? Or punish us? I pray about that every day. God considers us human for our souls. People who have lost it cease to be human in his eyes. And as for the revival of the Orthodox faith in Russia, I will tell you this. The candle has replaced the Komsomol badge, which hardly guarantees devotion to Christianity. And means only loyalty to the President. So if the candles are a mere formality, then those who hold them are the real Pharisees, the ones who will burn forever.

Our people are incredibly patient and at the same time very perceptive. Do you know what they now call the big bosses in Russia who stand in churches on the High Holidays? Candleholders! Whether these "candleholders" believe in God or not, only He knows. One thing is clear: the people do not see their sincerity, which is the point.

- But that is better than frenzied atheism, don't you think?

- Yes, with one correction. Those who believed in God during Soviet times were true believers. Now it's all hypocrisy. If you ask me, the bitter truth is better than sweet lies. And you can't fool God. You don't have to love God. First of all, you should love yourself and your close people, because God does not need love. People believe in God and fear his punishment! This is the point. Fear the punishment of heaven! For lack of fear of the Almighty brings great disasters to mankind, turning them into a deranged, dissolute mob of murderers. Fear can keep the soul from sin, and fear is stronger than the craving for evil. The law can only be established through fear, the full title of which is the fear of God. We must fear the power of the Almighty, for it is hidden and invisible.

- But this does not cancel out the injustice on earth... Why did my friends die? What was the need for their deaths? Why do innocent people die?

- Joseph, never say that God is unjust. For if he were unjust, he would have punished you long ago. We are all sinners and live in sin.

- You can't imagine how hard it is for me, Father Georgy... Close friends, even relatives, on opposite sides of the barricades, becoming enemies... I can't understand it, I can't accept it. Why is it like this...? - Joseph's voice trembled with emotional stress. - It was frightening to think that in the Soviet Union, where nations were forced to love each other so much, as soon as there was an opportunity, everything turned into mutual hate. And everyone had his or her own weighty, deep motives for that.

- You, Joseph, left the country at a very young age and may not have understood what was going on. What did the Soviets do? Under the "divide and rule" principle, they voluntarily drew borders on the traditional regions of non-Russian nationalities, creating the ground for numerous ethnic conflicts which, with the beginning of perestroika, took violent forms. So all the preconditions, as I said, were created at the dawn of the communist era.

Perestroika loosened the central government's control over the media and called it transparency. I remember reading sensational publications about the Stalinist clique's heinous crimes against its own people. There was a whiff of freedom in the air, and almost simultaneously with these new trends in the country, ethnic conflicts began: events in Ferghana, Nagorno-Karabakh, Tajikistan, Abkhazia, Moldova, and the Baltics. You see, the geography is vast, but the processes are the same: rampant separatism or striving for independence - whatever you want to call it. Fortunately, we have never had any restrictions in terms of terminology.

In the end, after a wave of murders and violence, one of the sides had a clear advantage and seemed to achieve some success, expressed in the proclamation of separate states - Abkhazia, Ossetia, Nagorno-Karabakh, and Transnistria. At the same time, all three republics, which included these newfound autonomies, remained as if they had lost. But in any case, this Pyrrhic victory did not resolve or even smoothen out the contradictions. Unresolved, it seems, was also part of the plans of the great combinators at the helm of power, and it gradually passed to the status of smoldering. Thus, the solution to the dispute moved from the fields of battle to the tables of all kinds of negotiations, which can take years or even decades. This is how it happens in real life. But the most striking thing is that after all the horrors of separatism, the organizers of these incidents are still occupying their positions! True, their positions have been renamed, but the winds of change have not thrown them out of their positions. They are still unsinkable. We can confidently say that these people, or their successors, continue to control the next stage of these conflicts, the frozen stage. Everything is proceeding as planned. Azerbaijan, Georgia, and Moldova, where the operations went almost perfectly, have been "cut off," and they are unable to rectify the situation without external support. Their own forces are insufficient for that. This was the idea of the organizers.

- Do you think that the modern Federal Security Service of Russia has the same power as the USSR State Security Committee (KGB) used to have?

--- "Perestroika" took away all-encompassing power from the Communist Party of the Soviet Union, but could not break the back of the KGB. This very tenacious organization has survived and continues to control absolutely everyone from the government to the homeless on the street. President Yeltsin had a chance to destroy the many-headed hydra, but he never took advantage of it. As well as in many other cases, his half-heartedness, indecision led to the fact that once again in Russia a unique opportunity was missed to completely cleance the country from the total, all-penetrating eye of the KGB. The repentance of government before the people did not take place. And the people apparently did not crave repentance.

- What are your hopes for newly elected President Putin? Little is known about him in the West.

- The new government, which outwardly looks like a successor from Yeltsin s government, actually came out again from the bowels of the same KGB. In Russian , the main state idea is the renewal of national-Chekism (chekism comes from the word Chekist, this is an organization created under Lenin, it was called a Checka, that is, an Emergency Commission, later converted into the KGB. This is what I foresee. Chekist came to power . And it is well known that Chekist remains a Chekist until the end of his life.

- Who were you in the worldly life before church? - Joseph wondered.

- I taught philosophy at Moscow State University. My dissertation was on Epicurus. When Russia was awakening, we all expected great changes, we thought that at last, the hour had come for Russia to purify itself, to repent for the past and move forward, to become a normal civilized European country, to shed its Asian stagnation and be completely free of the communist past. But life has shown that the brightest hopes were an illusion. The past is so strong that it will not let us go. It has not gone away; in its transformations, it holds sway over people's souls once again. Once again the people have been deceived. Yet they wanted to be deceived, because they didn't believe in change and didn't want it from the start. I got away from the hustle and bustle long before I realized it all...

- However, from the perspective of someone who has not been here for about twenty years, Russia has indeed become different. Especially evident is the religious upsurge, and there is much more freedom than in the Soviet Union.

- Yes, the change overthrew the old communist ideology and opened the door to Orthodoxy. Faith began to return to people's souls. Wounded, devastated, and desperate, they longed for fresh air, clean water, and light. The Church welcomed these servants of God into its bosom, helped them to endure the troubled times, persuaded them to drop their weapons, and kneel before the holy faces. It was then that I understood my purpose: to heal wounded souls with God's help, to help them to the best of my ability. At first, I studied at a theological seminary, then I was sent here as a priest. That's how I ended up in Rostov-on-Don.

- So where is Russia going now?

- Communist ideology lost its monopoly in 1991. After the collapse of the Soviet Union, the redistribution of property in Russia began. Now the security services are gaining power.

Thinking for a moment, the priest suddenly added:

- Look what the Russian language has been turned into! The very mighty and great language. It's stuffed with semi-gangster words and foreign borrowings. Remember what Solomon said: "Death and life are in the power of the tongue, and those who love it will enjoy its fruits. I also believe that the essence of human beings is determined by their speech.

- Yes, yes, it is very noticeable even in the immigrant community. Russian-speaking emigrants, having lived abroad for ten or even twenty years, still cannot fully fit into a foreign environment, they live in their past. They say it's because of the other environment and culture, but in reality, it's all about language! - Joseph confirmed Father's reasoning.

- Truly, "the verb is good. I understand what goes on in the soul and mind of a Russian person. During these ten to fifteen years, everything in them is mixed up, they are tired and want to rest, and at the same time, they are pulled back. The Soviet mythology is bursting at the seams, and all the ideals of the past have lost their significance: the one-party system is no longer relevant, Stalin is worse than Hitler, Lenin is a German spy and the founder of the first concentration camps, Makhno is a highly educated man, and Bandera is a fighter for the happiness of the Ukrainian people. But people are nostalgic for the old times, and nothing can be done about it. For the Russian people, at least for the majority, such concepts as strong statehood, majesty, and Motherland, are primary and more understandable than liberal freedoms and personal initiative. Alexander II abolished slavery in Russia, but they did not place a single monument to him in his homeland. They even threw a bomb at him - why? Under Soviet rule, the psychology of equality and fear was inculcated, to be replaced by the psychology of inequality and envy. Yes, they do not like the happy and rich in Russia!

Joseph listened in amazement to the musings of the man sitting before him in the dark cassock of a clergyman. He could hardly have time to digest so much new information, much was an absolute revelation to him.

- Father Georgy, you impressed me...

- Of course! You have a completely different world over there in America. And Russia should be studied through the research of monasteries. All Russian culture came out of the monastery. That's where ethics and the concept of conscience come from. In Russia, all moral categories are radical and serious. To understand this country, one must learn what Orthodoxy is.

- Consequently, the choice of Orthodoxy as the state religion largely predetermined the future fate of Russia?

- Absolutely right! In fact, it could not be otherwise. The Slavs could not become Catholics by definition. They are different from the Europeans. And they wouldn't be Muslims either, because they are different from the Middle Eastern Asians. So something in between was chosen - Orthodoxy. The Byzantine-Greek model of Christianity corresponded to the Slavic spirit. And what is Byzantism? It is, unfortunately, the kingdom of intrigue, deceit, and hypocrisy. This is the legacy we have received. But many of those who are concerned about power have no idea that power, according to its original definition, is just a ball, which was held during coronation and other high ceremonies by Byzantine emperors, and later by Russian tsars. I am convinced that the nation itself, its soul, creates its history, its destiny, creating or borrowing traditions and customs close to it in spirit, as well as reforming religion according to its spiritual needs.

Let us take Christianity as an example. How many different denominations of this seemingly single religious doctrine have spread to other countries? Typically, the states with the highest standard of living and democratic freedoms are those that practice Protestantism: Holland, Denmark, England, Germany, the United States, Canada, Australia, and New Zealand. Catholic countries are in second place: France, Italy, Spain, and so on. Orthodox countries are in third place: Greece, Russia, Bulgaria, and others.

- Do you think Russia needs Protestantism? - Joseph raised his eyebrows in surprise. He was more and more amazed by this unusual man, who spoke such strange words in the orthodox monastery.

- Well, it is ridiculous and foolish to talk about the mass acceptance of the Protestant ethic by Russians now. But I firmly believe that all thieving and economically poor nations need it like air. Indeed! Someone said that Protestants sit with God at the same table. Catholics and Orthodox are different: their God is at an unreachable height, and human beings are nobodies, nothing. It's like the Scriptures, "I am the worm. This self-perception has become part of the mentality, and it is hard to change.

- It's the opposite with Americans. They do not understand how it is possible to suffer from hunger, cold, and lack of shelter and still get drunk, steal, and look for enemies among real laborers, savvy entrepreneurs, and non-Americans. Americans are used to relying on their own resources for everything, Joseph put in.

- Because Americans don't know our history and don't understand that for centuries, Russian society has been based on a communal culture and psychology, has rejected any kind of individualism, and has seen higher justice in equality, including economic equality. For a Protestant American, by contrast, individualism means that each person stands for himself and God stands for everybody, Father Georgy countered.

- Excuse me, but it is very unusual to hear such a speech from an Orthodox priest... The priest of the church, the guest said.

- Yes, it must seem very strange to others. Sometimes I contradict myself. But I have an excuse. First, I'm talking to an American who was born on our land. And secondly, I'm a kind of... dissident priest.

- And you don't have any problems with the religious hierarchy?

- So far I haven't.

After a short pause, Father Georgy continued his reasoning:

- I have always wondered why in Orthodoxy the closest person to sainthood is the poor, the beggar, the destitute. Not the one who works, who creates and builds, but the one who begs for alms! Why does Orthodoxy consider this world a place of sorrow and suffering? I myself certainly believe that we came to this earth to suffer, because without suffering it is impossible to know the meaning of life. You cannot live righteously without repenting for the sins you commit. But on the other hand, if you think about it, life itself is a gift from the Almighty and should be treated as a great blessing. It is this Protestant optimism that we need for our rebirth!

Inside the Russian person - no matter whether he is a lord, a peasant, or a serf - there always sits a small, bad demon of passive anarchism, who inspires in us a careless and indifferent attitude to work, to society, to the people, to ourselves. I am more and more convinced every day that the morality of Protestantism could help us overcome this demon. If, of course, we wish to overcome it.

- Do you really believe this is possible? After all, Protestant ethics presupposes individualism, personal initiative, faith in one's own strength, restraint, discipline, and so on. As far as I understand, these are qualities that are strange to the Russian character.

- I am well aware that any faith comes gradually, without its being imposed by force. And every nation is worthy not only of its leader but also of its religion. But this is the problem! I believe in one God, his son Jesus Christ, and the Holy Spirit. I love my poor people and wish them nothing but good. But if I see something good in Protestantism, Puritan morality, or Buddhist writings, for example, I believe we are worthy to benefit from these holy gifts.

I realize that by nature our people are mostly conservative, inert, and not inclined to make quick and dramatic changes. The entire history of my nation is various kinds of experiments on itself, where all changes were introduced exclusively by violent means and never by evolutionary means. Our people have become stubborn, rigid, and hard to change peacefully, including religiously. They have always been used as cannon fodder or they have been destroyed.

Now it is reasonable to ask, who will hear my message and who will believe me? Especially now, when most people are more convinced than ever that any, even the best wishes if they come from people who believe in Western values, are always harmful to the Russian people. They say that the Western way and Western values are a threat. And I say, is the love of labor, the ability to work, a strong family, the ability to rely on your own strength, taking initiative - good only for the West?

Joseph looked questioningly at Father, not interrupting him. Noticing his confusion, the priest stopped talking and grinned bitterly:

- Yes, I understand how unusual it is for you to hear those words. But I try not to be deceitful, neither when I speak to my flock nor now, before you. People who understand the importance of these values need to take at least some steps in that direction. Well, I don't know how to explain it... The great Sakharov said: "We need victory over chaos, over

Russian chaos." It's like overcoming entropy. This is what should drive our best minds: the overcoming of chaos, both in social relations and within each of us.

Because the inner overcoming of chaos is the pursuit of freedom. And freedom is the highest moral and ethical value in general, including in Protestantism. I repeat these words every day. People, cherish freedom, for it is the only thing worth cherishing. Nothing in this life is as cheap or as costly as true freedom. And Sakharov also taught that freedom is a system of inner limitations. And internal restrictions are the Ten Commandments given to people by the Almighty. So, the circle closed. Maybe Russia will still be fine. It is a relatively young country.

- Why do you think so?

- Because it started its monotheism only a thousand years ago.

- Frankly speaking, I never associated the maturity of people with the time of accepting a monotheistic religion. Although there is something interesting about it... - Joseph said thoughtfully.

- Summing up our conversation, I want to add that there are two main scourges in Russia: Asian stagnation and Byzantine worldview. Because of them, all reforms toward supposed Europeanization have been failing for more than five hundred years. But the achievements cannot be denied, if we turn a blind eye to the price they have been achieved at.

Reforms are usually imposed from above by the top of the pyramid - the power - tsarist, Soviet, and presidential. And it never completes them. First of all, it cannot completely cut off the bough on which it sits. Secondly, the population of Russia, which is under the influence of the Byzantine worldview, is fundamentally rigidly Asian. What do dissenting voices, dissidents, and democrats want? They want power, they want political and economic change. The only difference in principle is that they are trying to make these reforms more painful, faster, and more decisive in order to achieve the cherished goal of Europeanization of the country. But as long as these two scourges define the mentality of the majority, reforms will be powerless every time.

I will say again, of course, in the last five hundred years we have seen progress, very slow progress, but still progress. And the price to pay for it is great! And for political and economic reforms to really "go" and for the price to be adequate, a SPIRITUAL REVOLUTION is needed. This does not require politicians. You need people of the Russian clergy who think in reformist terms! They must bring change in the souls of people, as Luther and Calvin did in their time in Europe, the religious revolution, that is the Reformation - without a single shot being fired and without a mountain of corpses. This is what Russia needs! Breaking the Asian stagnation and freeing the soul from its Byzantine heritage.

Puritanism is the only great creation of the late period of Christian religious history. The Age of Enlightenment in Western Europe was of English origin and was the result of puritanism. I would even say that the West is now so powerful because of it. Of course, in Russia, it may take more, many years... But we have to start somewhere!

Father Georgy spoke with such fervor and conviction that Joseph had no choice but to agree with him.

- Of course, Joseph, you know better. But I think there's a bit of a crisis of Protestant ethics in America itself, isn't there?

- Yes, unfortunately. WASP1 is now representative of the outgoing, old, provincial America that I love so much. It's devout, it helps the poor, it's honest, and there's a strong belief in a human being's word.

(1 English abbreviation for "White Anglo-Saxon Protestant,")

- I think liberals and their values are, ironically enough, to blame for the demise of this classic America. The modern America that religious people don't like is the fault of liberals. I believe that the America of our day needs a revitalization of Protestant fundamentalism, neo-Puritanism, as the only way to save dying humanity. At the center of this ethic is the cult of work as a daily prayer to God, as an end in itself. And the cult of the family. Otherwise, Western civilization risks repeating the fate of the Roman Empire, which at one point became defenseless in the face of a barbarian invasion.

Three hours of conversation with the clergyman flew by unnoticed for Joseph, crushed by the weight of grief and physically exhausted.

- Excuse me, Joseph, will you have one free evening in Moscow? I would like to ask you - if you don't mind, of course - to arrange a meeting with Academician Yakushev.

- Yakushev? - Joseph asked again. - Who's that?

- Oh, right, Father Georgy smiled understandingly, you left in the early eighties and never heard of him. He was one of the chief architects of perestroika, the chief ideologist of the Gorbachev era.

- Would such a man really agree to talk to me? - Joseph said doubtfully.

- Well, first of all, he retired a long time ago, and secondly, he is my friend, concluded the priest proudly, continuing to smile. Then he got serious and added: First of all, Alexander Yakushev is a very interesting conversationalist. If he has some free time, you will really enjoy it. He can tell you firsthand, so to speak, what happened in the late eighties and early nineties. I am referring to the collapse of the Union and, accordingly, the death of tens of thousands of people, including your friends.

With these words, the priest handed Joseph a piece of paper with a telephone number on it. Then he blessed him and let him go in peace.

Chapter 10

Joseph was flying to Moscow on an old Tu-154, but, feeling the loss of his friends gravely, he did not notice his discomfort. As soon as the plane gained altitude, he fell asleep in his seat: the stress of the previous day had taken its toll. He was awakened by the jolts accompanying the landing at Domodedovo airport.

It was late evening in Moscow. Two hours later Joseph entered the Metropolitan Hotel, where a room had been reserved for him. Tiredness did not go away, his head kept hurting. He took a shower and went to bed, but could not fall asleep for a long time. He kept thinking about what had so unexpectedly happened to him these days.

In the morning Joseph was awakened by a cell phone alarm. He opened his eyes with difficulty. For the first seconds, he didn't even know where he was. But as soon as his consciousness cleared, sleepiness vanished like as if by magic. He jumped out of bed, washed his face quickly, went out to the buffet for breakfast, and called Armen's brother.

After several beeps Joseph heard a voice with a strong Armenian accent:

- Hello, who do you need?

- Hello, I'm looking for Karen.

There was a little fuss, and the voice of another man came through:

- I'm Karen. Who's calling?

- Karen, this is Joseph, a childhood friend of Armen's. I came all the way from New York...

- Joseph, is that you?! Of course, I remember you! It's great that you came, brother. I'm so glad to hear you.

- Can we meet right now?

- Yeah, sure. Could you drive up to our place? Where are you?

- I'm at the Metropolitan Hotel. Tell me the address.

Joseph decided to take a walk for a while. He was curious to see Moscow. He walked down Tverskaya Street, went down to the Red Square, crossed the Alexander Garden, and then headed in the direction of Old Arbat. The historic part of the city was almost unchanged. But its spirit was different, and not just because ultra-modern stores and luxury restaurants occupied all the first floors of ancient buildings. It seemed to Joseph that the people themselves had changed. These Moscow people were different from those who remained in his youthful memories.

Going into a cafe at Old Arbat, Joseph had a quick bite to eat, went out to Kalininsky Avenue, where he caught there a taxi, and headed for Karen's place.

Armen's brother lived near the Babushkinskaya metro station. It was a nice, green part of the capital. Soviet-era high-rises lined the road.

The door was opened by a stocky young man of short stature, with black long hair and a large, hooked nose.

- Karen, it's for you! - he shouted as he said hello. Then he held out his hand and introduced himself: Misha.

- Joseph.

They shook hands.

- Come in. Karen will be right out.

The guest walked along the corridor and came into the room. Karen stepped toward him from the adjoining room with outstretched arms.

Having met Armen's brother on the street, Joseph, of course, would not have recognized him. Standing in front of him was a tall, handsome guy with short-cut dark brown hair. His face was somehow subtly reminiscent of his brother. They embraced.

- Could it really be you, Karen? - Joseph exhaled.

- Yes, it is me. Have a seat on the sofa. You've changed too, Joseph, Karen remarked, taking the chair opposite.

- Karen, I already know everything. Been to Baku.

- Yes, Armen... - And Karen was silent, embarrassed, and lowered his eyes to the floor. - We haven't even found his body to give him a proper burial. Armen has been reported missing, he added quietly.

Joseph felt drops of sweat break out on his forehead. He wrapped his cold hands around Karen's head and pressed his forehead against it.

- Have you heard about Volodya?

- No, I don't know anything about him.

- He was killed in the Chechen war.

- What are you saying?! Oh no... He was such a great guy...

- That's it... I came back after eighteen years to see my friends, and they were taken away from me. Tell me, why, why was life so cruel? Why did my friends die? What was their fault?

- Wait! We know what Armen died for! He died defending the Armenian land of Artsakh from those Azerbaijani subhumans! - Misha spoke arrogantly.

Joseph looked at him tiredly and noticed the anger and hatred glowing in his eyes. Then he turned his gaze to Karen, somewhat embarrassed by this statement, and said:

- Karen, I need some fresh air. I don't feel well... Please, walk me out.

- Yes, of course, if you need to go out, I'm here for you. Once outside, Joseph hurriedly apologized:

- I'm sorry for the way I acted. But it was hard for me to stay there, in the company of your friend...

- Yeah, he's a passionate patriot.

- Look, take me to some quiet place so we can sit quietly and commemorate our boys. Memories are all we have left.

After catching the car, Karen drove Joseph to a Greek tavern. It was about three o'clock. It was a weekday, and most of the tables were unoccupied. The tavern was very cozy. Quiet music was pouring in from somewhere on the walls and ceiling. A waiter quickly set the table, and Joseph poured the vodka into shot glasses.

- I want to drink in memory of my friends! God has sent me a trial, he has taken away three people close to me. After all these years of separation, I have come here only to find out that they died a long time ago...? How could it be...? What a cruel world, what a terrible time we live in! And if there is a heavenly kingdom, may they meet there, Joseph finished his toast with his head bowed.

Poor Karen's eyes moistened, and he could no longer hold back his tears. One drop after another slid down his cheeks.

- Yes, Joseph, such a tragedy has occurred in our family... Can you imagine what Asya felt when she lost her husband and brother? And our parents? What can I say? - Karen emptied his glass in a gulp and wiped his wet eyes with a napkin.

- Do you live in Moscow all the time?

- Yes, I am a Russian citizen and I do business here. We opened an outerwear store.

- How is it going?

- So-so, with varying success. We're trying to do as much as we can. Of course, it's not easy.

- I see you're not married.

- No. Are you?

- Neither am I.

- Why not?

- I don't have time for this.

- What do you do?

- I work as a manager in a large investment company, - modestly answered Joseph. - We invest money in profitable industries, including oil and gas. How are things in Armenia?

- You probably know that even though Armenia won the war with Azerbaijan, it is actually under an economic blockade. It does not have very warm relations with Georgia. The only "friend" that has common borders with us, so to speak, is Iran. We are friends with Iran. But the best relations are with Russia. We have a military agreement, and you know, this is a serious thing. Russian troops guard the border with Turkey. The United States also helps. American Armenians lobby for our political and financial interests. I think Armenia would be in trouble without their help.

- And what about the people?

- What about the people? They are always scapegoats. And how many of them are left in Armenia? About two and a half million. In search of a better life, Armenians are still moving to Russia. They don't really want to die fighting with Azerbaijan. We have a huge diaspora here, about two million, and another four million in other countries, including the USA, France, Syria, and so on.

- Why do you think Azerbaijan was defeated in the Karabakh war?

- What do you mean by "why"? Because we were right! But we should not forget that the Russians helped us a lot.

- Karen, I didn't have a chance to see Rafik's daughter, so please take this check to the bearer. Just don't get too angry! It's for the baby.

Joseph held out the envelope.

- I'm leaving in a day. But I'll be busy tomorrow, so I won't be able to see them. Well, goodbye and kiss the baby for me! And also, I really ask you to keep in touch with Rafik's mother. Make sure she will meet her granddaughter. Do you promise?

- Of course I promise, Joseph-Jan! And they hugged each other.

Chapter 11

The next day Joseph called Academician Yakushev, who invited him to his apartment for a meeting.

The owner opened the door himself. He was a big, fat, gray-haired man, who looked tired - the years were taking their toll after all. His face seemed permanently imprinted with an immense burden of responsibility, but his perceptive eyes were still sparkling with wit. He looked straight ahead, unblinking, trying to get into his interlocutor's innermost thoughts. They walked down the spacious hallway to a large square room. This was Yakushev's office. All the walls here, from bottom to top, were covered with shelves full of books. There were pictures and family photographs hanging in the small gaps in the walls. Among them, Joseph discerned pictures of the academician with Gorbachev and the leaders of foreign countries. A huge desk was by the window. To the right, in the corner, there were massive armchairs, a sofa, and a table. The old oak parquet was carefully cleaned and shiny. The room was decorated with many statuettes and vases brought from various countries.

Alexander Nikolayevich invited Joseph to sit down in an armchair, and he himself took a seat opposite. Between them, there was only a low, massive mahogany coffee table.

- What would you like to drink - tea, coffee, juices, or something stronger? Joseph asked for a cup of coffee.

- Katya! Katya! - Alexander Nikolayevich called out loudly.

After a while, the door opened, and a middle-aged, pretty woman in a pink apron stood on the threshold.

- Do you need anything, Alexander Nikolaevich? - she asked, and seeing Joseph, nodded her head.

- Yes, Katya. Please, coffee for our guest, and a cup of tea for me.

After some common phrases, Joseph briefly talked about what he had experienced during the past few days.

- Yeah, well... Everything you've told me is terrible, but unfortunately, these are the lessons we had to go through. Sure, there have been mistakes and kinks and somebody's dirty schemes, but that's the abyss we've fallen into. Now we have to climb out; not to keep it hidden, not to obscure it, not to lurk - but to come out with an open face.

- Everything remains as it was. Have any of the interethnic conflicts that arose with the collapse of the Soviet Union been resolved? No! It was frozen at best.

- Yes, you're right. It's easy to fan the flames of hate, but very hard to extinguish them. This kind of inter-ethnic and inter-religious strife is still a tight knot that cannot be untangled. After the collapse of the Soviet Union, dog-eat-dog laws came to the forefront. The more powerful, shrewd, prepared, and lucky have more chances to win. In times like these, these qualities become decisive. In contrast, the concepts of state protection, social justice, and the rule of law become profane or don't work at all.

- And yet I think that too high a price has been paid for the situation in which the peoples of the former Soviet Union find themselves today.

- My dear Joseph, of course, in human terms you are a thousand times right! Of course, any social and political cataclysms or attempts to implement even the noblest ideas almost always come at an exorbitant price. Did you know that this miserable country lost tens of millions of citizens for the right to be called the Soviet Union? That was the price for the opportunity to build a communist society.

The door opened, and Katya came in with a large tray. She put beautiful cloth napkins on the table and served cups and bowls with candies, fruits, and desserts. All her movements were quick, beautiful, and elegant.

- Thank you, Katya, - Yakushev smiled warmly.

- You're welcome, Alexander Nikolayevich. - She left the room, shutting the door tightly.

- So, Joseph, please don't be shy and try our treats. I like when people eat from the heart! You know, my doctors forbid me, but I believe fifty grams of cognac won't make a difference.

With those words, he got up, went to the bar, opened the bar door, and took out a bottle of Armenian cognac.

- My friends sent me this from Armenia. They say it is very different from what you find in the stores. To be honest, I'm not a big connoisseur. But let's try it!

He put two small crystal glasses on the table and filled them. At once a sweet and peculiar smell entered the room.

- Dear Joseph, let's commemorate your deceased friends! May their memory live on, and their lives and deaths serve as a lesson and example for the younger generation. They fought for their homeland, each in his own way, sometimes on different sides of the barricades. And yet, each of them performed their soldierly duty, despite what politicians, military and special services did behind their backs. These guys were honest before their people. Eternal memory and glory to them!

After a short silence, Joseph continued:

- Okay, I can understand everything: the collapse of a huge country, the consequences of its agony... But the Karabakh conflict began in 1988, and people, citizens of one country, started to fight with each other. Where was the Soviet government? Why did they let it happen? This is what my mind refuses to understand!

- You're right, Joseph. But everything that came out then goes back to the deep past. If you want to know, I personally was accused by some individuals of fomenting separatism in Armenia, alluding to the Karabakh events. Of course, I agree, that for everything that happened in the country during those years, including interethnic discord, the responsibility is on the country's leadership, on Gorbachev and me as well. I do not absolve myself of the blame in this regard. But it is absolutely wrong to blame the blood in Baku, Vilnius, Tbilisi, Alma-Ata and other "trouble spots " only on Gorbachev. All these ideas were drummed into people's heads by the State Committee on the State of Emergency, who are now trying to absolve themselves of blame for many of their provocations that ended in bloodshed. Gorbachev himself said that national conflicts cannot be resolved by force. But the security services were thirsty for blood, spilled it, and then reported that weapons were used only as a retaliatory measure.

Moreover, the security services, scared of perestroika, provoked riots and conflict situations themselves in order to prove their usefulness. This was the case in Alma-Ata, Fergana, Sumgayit, Baku, Vilnius and Riga. But on the other hand, the former republics themselves craved autonomous power. As a result of nationalist demagogy, we got wars and conflicts, the desire to kill someone and avenge something. Separatism is a terrible thing. It can lead any society to a dead-end of conflicts between all of them.

- Alexander Nikolayevich, you were at the origins of perestroika. Now, after ten to fifteen years, how do you assess what happened? Do you regret anything that you've done or if you could, would you do it all over again?

- Well, first of all, I openly confessed and repented of mistakes I had made. How could I avoid it? If I had known where to fall, I would have put a straw on the ground. But generally speaking, I do not regret anything. Secondly, if I had to do it all over again, I'd just consider past mistakes. We wanted to change our country - not to destroy it, note you! - We wanted to change it, to make it open and free, to show people where the truth is and where the lies are. We wanted them to learn how to work and get decent money for it. We wanted them to understand that they could determine their own fate. But, unfortunately, all attempts to reform the social structure failed. I see the main reason for this in the conservative, inert psychology of our people. I agree, under tsarism, until 1861, there was a slave system. But along with this, there was, albeit not widespread, but the rule of law and legal consciousness. During the first decades of its existence, the Soviet regime destroyed advocacy as an instrument to protect individual rights, since they did not exist in the Soviet Union. Along with the advocate's role, jurisprudence was brought down and a crushing blow was dealt to the part of the human consciousness responsible for obeying the law. As a result, the possession of power did not become synonymous with adherence to the law. For the Soviet people, the concepts of democracy, rights, morality, and justice lost their meaning and power forever. Fear, disbelief, godlessness and hypocrisy were firmly rooted in us. Besides, Russia prefers not freedom, but will, which means "anarchy" - whatever I want, I will do it. In the civilized world, freedom means, first of all, responsibility and commitment. But in Russia, when a person gets power, he does what he wants, not what he has to do.

- You know, Alexander Nikolaevich, I noticed that in Russia, and in Azerbaijan and, apparently, in other former Soviet republics too, people, calling themselves democrats or national democrats, are unable to come to an agreement among themselves. Then how can you condemn ordinary citizens who do not trust them? Why is it that people who proclaim democratic principles always have more personal ambition than common sense?

- You are very observant, young man! And you know, it doesn't depend on age. Old and young advocates of individual rights and freedoms fight among themselves like cats and dogs.

- Why do former Soviet intellectuals who call themselves democrats have so much selfishness and ambition? - Joseph asked again.

- I think it's because they also were born among the common people and are not very different from ordinary people. One might say, the difference is only in education, ideology and civility, which turn out to be trashy and superficial. Our "intelligentsia" has always been very amenable to the charms of power. The great Nabokov once compared the Soviet "intelligentsia" to courtiers talking about the landlord. They would gather in the stable and cluck, but when their master called, they would run to serve.

The same thing is happening today. In Russia today, authoritarianism is beating liberalism, and there is much credit for this to be given to our homegrown intellectual "elite," which is more capable than anyone else of adapting to rigid frames. On the other hand, the authorities always cultivate conformism, this special kind of civilized slavery. The tragedy of modern Russia lies precisely in the intellectual and psychological conformism of our political elite. So it's all about the people themselves, in each and every one of us.

We wanted freedom, but it turns out that no one wants it. We do not know it and do not know how to use it. Who are we? People who rat on their neighbors, who are happy to see that someone was punished. Some snitching, others keeping quiet... Who was working in the punitive authorities? The kind of people who were villains? No, just ordinary people. So who are we? Until we answer this question, we won't succeed in building anything in Russia. All of society, from head to toe, needs to repent. We were the ones who tried to trample or kill others, we tortured and murdered our own kind, we snitched, denounced and stigmatized them at various meetings. Snitching was considered an honorable thing to do. So we were all to blame. A part of society is convinced that Lenin was a villain. But then who are they themselves?

Now we are building a strong country. But somehow it turns out to be a dictatorship - a bureaucracy! Society is being drugged by a game of patriotism, and no one understands what a powerful state should really be like. And first of all, it should be free, rich, independent and not malicious person.

- So what kind of sphinx is Russia? Not the West and not the East. Something in between or on its own?

- Everyone is obsessed with Western civilization. In my opinion, there are no Western or Eastern ideals in the world anymore. There is civilization or barbarism. The myth about the special Russian way, God's chosenness and the mysterious soul is very expensive for Russia. Peter the Great's Preobrazhensky regiment, Alexander I, Alexander II's Freemasons and Lenin's Commissars tried to put an end to the so-called "special Russian way", but the stubborn Russian hardheadedness is ready to undermine itself rather than unite with the rest of civilized humanity.

Russia has to understand that there is no "special Russian way," it's an illusion. Just as there is no special Chinese or American way.

With all the variety of cultural halftones, there is one and only way out - the liberal-democratic way. All countries must inevitably join the process of globalization, otherwise, they will only be raw appendages of civilized countries.

In the post-industrial world, knowledge and the people who possess it are the driving force of economic growth. And if Russia needs some kind of super-idea - which I am not sure it does - it is on the surface, general, without deviation or backtracking. It is a war on poverty! The most just of wars! Thus, there is no need to clog heads with metaphysical speculation: Russia's true problems lie on the surface - poverty, and disenfranchisement. Poverty arises from the absence of private property. The reason for disenfranchisement arises from the exaggerated, inordinate importance of the state in public life. Do Russians want a national idea? Please, it's Freedom, Prosperity, and Justice.

- Here I could argue with you because this is not a national idea, but a universal one.

- And what's wrong with that, if there's only benefits? Freedom and the material well-being of citizens can make society decent and the state respectable. Freedom is the only way to save Russia. The new government is trying to build a strong state. But what is that? For example, is Sweden a strong state?

Alexander Nikolayevich made a significant pause and stared at Joseph, who nodded his head slightly perplexed.

- Yes, it's a free and rich country. What do the current governors want? For Russia to be powerful with the tyranny of government officials, missiles, nuclear weapons, repression, and poor people? No way! We have been through all this before. Officials need freedom from responsibility, so they can rob and destroy people.

For a moment Yakushev leaned back, his eyelids half-closed as if to give himself a break from his emotional outburst.

- I can deduce from your words that Russian society is not yet ready for repentance. And repentance is also the way to freedom, a kind of deliverance from the evil past.

- In our country, it is the exact opposite. Look at the attitudes of our society. Maksimilian Voloshin's words come to mind: "Yesterday's slave, tired of freedom, will revolt, demanding chains". This is the exact characteristic of the spiritual condition of today's Russia.

- Yet it remains a mystery to me why so many people are still nostalgic about Stalin and his era.

- You see, the thing is... Stalin is a very contradictory and complicated person. I would call him a great villain. People's memory is mostly short, and bad things are forgotten quickly. But everyone remembers the greatness of the empire led by the "father of nations". Besides, elderly people consider themselves doomed to live out their old age in poverty, and sometimes in misery, that is, abandoned to the mercy of fate. Stalin and his era have become, as it were, an alternative to modern life; back then, in their minds, the elderly of today actually lived rather than shamefully eking out an existence. This is the only way to explain the motives of the people who still carry Stalin's portraits at demonstrations. Otherwise, worshipping the leader is mental blindness and deafness, in other words, ignorance. I might add that human beings were created in such a way that, for some reason, the past always seems better than the present; the sun shone brighter and the sky glowed more bluely in earlier years. You see, Joseph, in fact, everything is simple and, at the same time, difficult to achieve. After all, if people are smart and hardworking, their state will prosper. This trivial equation is what makes up the nation's greatness.

The conversation with Academician Yakushev made an indelible impression on Joseph. He was able to see one of the last bisons of a bygone era. He was probably the only man of his magnitude who had repented of his communist past and tried to turn the country's back on a thousand years of slavery in order to behold the dawn of a free future.

Chapter 12

Late that night, a Boeing 747 was taking Joseph to America. Slowly sipping whiskey, the young man tried to sort out his feelings. In the United States, his life had been relatively smooth, albeit a little harsh, but always stable. Everything in it was almost ninety percent predictable, and all that was required of him was compliance, diligence, faith in his abilities, and some intellectual expenditure. In his former homeland, Joseph experienced the shock of killer news and the atmosphere of hopelessness that overtook him everywhere he went. He was shocked to the core by the circumstances that led to the deaths of his friends. Joseph's emotional threshold was too low to understand and accept everything. As a result, he had a nervous breakdown, of which he was not yet aware because he was in a constant state of tension. As he began to relax little by little, he gradually slipped into the abyss of severe depression.

Upon arriving home, Joseph called the office and told them he was feeling unwell and would be absent from work for several days. Then he started experiencing unbearable headaches. His body refused to obey and seemed broken, his interest in life and work had been lost. Joseph locked himself away, did not want to see anyone, did not answer the phone, and would not allow his parents to come from Florida to visit him. The only person in the house was the housekeeper, who cleaned, grocery-shopped, and cooked. There was no appetite, and the man lost a significant amount of weight over the week. He stopped taking care of himself and did not go out. Friends and coworkers, to whom he listlessly answered the phone, urged him to see doctors and psychoanalysts, but all in vain. Indifference to everything became total. Joseph secluded himself in his bedroom and for hours stared fixedly at the ceiling.

It was the eighth day of his voluntary confinement, and during that time Joseph could not sleep normally. Inward tension did not allow him to relax. All these nights he spent in a half-slumber, distinguishing even the night rustles and sounds outside the window. Each time dusk began a new round of torment. It was not even insomnia, but a kind of delirium. He was delirious, and it was torture. He met every morning exhausted and broken.

This night was no different from previous nights. It was a full moon. The curtains on the windows remained open. There was a huge, round moon hanging right in front of eyes, brightly illuminating the bedroom.

Sometimes Joseph's eyelids fluttered open slightly, and he could not only discern noises, but he could see everything around him. At first, he thought he had finally really fallen asleep, as he hadn't slept yet since his return. But something was wrong with this dream he was having... This "something" made Joseph open his eyes wide and clearly see some people three meters away from him. He was not even frightened, did not scream, did not jump to his feet, but continued to watch them with amazement.

The strangers looked unusual, for they were dressed in white robes reminiscent of ancient tunics or togas. He remembered that such clothes had been worn in the days of ancient Greece and Rome. There were four of them, all men. Three with beards and mustaches.

Joseph looked closely at the one without facial hair: he looked like a Hindu. Another resembled an Arab; the other two looked like Hasidic Jews from Borough Park.

(1 The neighborhood of Brooklyn, where mostly Orthodox Jews live.)

Joseph rubbed his eyes once more and pinched himself to make sure he was awake, but he still lay there.

Finally, the oldest of the strangers, the man with the long beard, stepped forward and spoke in plain English:

- Honorable Joseph, we are glad to welcome you into our society.

- Who are you? - Joseph said, but he did not hear his own voice, though he was sure that he had spoken the words.

- The messengers of the Almighty, Buddha, Mohammed, Jesus, and I, Moses, are before you.

It was only now that Joseph realized, to his amazement, that the greatest religious prophets and even the son of God, Jesus Christ, were standing in front of him.

- Why should I be so honored? - he could only whisper.

- Brother, we are here to tell you that you are chosen as our next messenger by our Supreme Creator, who created all things visible and invisible. Your predecessor was our venerable brother Mohammed, who delivered God's word to people thirteen centuries ago. Now listen to us attentively.

The whole history of mankind is its way to the Creator. And we see how difficult that way has been, is, and will continue to be for mankind.

You know how it all began. Our Creator first chose the Jewish people and revealed Himself to them first through Abraham, telling them whom they should obey and whom they should pray to. Then the Almighty appeared to me and handed me the Tablets with the Ten Commandments. It was the law by which my people were to live. Otherwise, the Jews were going to perish. But for the next three thousand years, they behaved too unwisely, often breaking God's commandments, with the result that God allowed Israel's enemies to scatter its twelve tribes and take away the Holy Land, given from above.

Time passed. God chose a new messenger, Jesus of Nazareth, and gave him His Word. The Jews considered this act as a betrayal of their Faith and their God by Jesus. They had no idea that their God was the God of all mankind, since there was no one else. The Jews thought that Jesus had turned from the righteous path and wanted to relegate people to heresy. But that was truly God's plan, the plan of the same God who gave me, Moses, the holy tablets, for there is no Creator but One God.

And that is what happened. Many Gentile nations were imbued with God's Word, His commandments, and most importantly, they became monotheists. This is how the different nations came to know God through Jesus Christ. This was God's plan: to open humanity's eyes, to inspire in their souls true faith in the One Creator. A few centuries later, the Almighty chose another messenger, the Honorable Muhammad, and gave him His Word for those peoples who still did not know about the existence of the One God.

What do we see now? Almost all of mankind believes in One Creator, but there are several religions in the world, each claiming the truth of its own God and pointing out the misguidance of the others. "There is no God but Allah" was once a great truth for the Gentiles in Arabia. But today the truth is clear: the Jewish God, the Christian God, Allah in Islam, and the Almighty, who brought enlightenment to the Venerable Buddha, are one and the same Creator, the One Creator of all that exists. We are all children of the same God, because the world is God, our Creator-Father. We are all parts of the same whole, whose center is the One Supreme who created us.

And you, dear brother Joseph, have been chosen by the Almighty to be God's new messenger. God has entrusted you with the mission of bringing to people what I have just told you, this absolute Truth, this Faith in the One and Undivided God of everyone and everything.

Joseph felt a fire flare up inside him. His whole body was burning hot: his hands, his face, his stomach, his feet-it seemed to him that he was about to ignite and burn. He was about to faint when the man who looked like Jesus approached and lightly touched his forehead with his palm. Joseph immediately felt the fever begin to subside and be replaced by a blissful coolness. He opened his eyes again. His body had not felt such an uplift for a long time. The prophets looked at their future companion with concern, as if waiting for an answer.

- But why me? he asked only with lips, as it seemed to Joseph. - You know that I am of Jewish descent, and not many people will listen to me.

- This is God's plan, and it is not for us to discuss it! - Moses exclaimed. - The Almighty have chosen you, as the representative of the Jewish people, to bear all the responsibility for the Faith in One God, because God first chose your people, rewarding them with faith in Himself.

- Yes, but how am I going to do that? I cannot... - he muttered fearfully.

- Yes, you can! God Himself has chosen you. Just like you, we were once ordinary people, and he chose us. Your mission on earth is to end all wars on earth! That is your primary mission.

- What? All wars?!

- Yes, you will convince the nations to stop fighting each other.

- But that... ...is fundamentally impossible.

- You can do it, Joseph. You can stop the mutual hatred of nations. People will finally realize that the Earth is their common home, given to them by the Almighty. Everything is in God's hands. Don't worry, brother. You will succeed, because you are God's chosen one.

After these words, Joseph fell back into a deep sleep and when he woke up, he heard the telephone ring. He could hardly open his eyes because he had been asleep for so long. The telephone went silent, and Joseph continued to lie there with his eyes open, staring at the ceiling.

Not a trace of the headache remained. His body seemed to be freed from some inner shackles that had been pressing down on him and preventing him from breathing in. Joseph felt an inner energy that he had never felt before. It was so powerful that he felt as if he could move mountains.

Suddenly the memory of an unusual dream hit him, and he remembered who he had been talking to and who he had seen. Abruptly he got out of bed and quickly paced the room.

"What was that? - He asked himself for the hundredth time. - Was it a dream or a reality? No, what am I talking about? What reality...? It was just a dream. But then how do I explain the changes that happened to me? I woke up a completely different person."

Joseph really felt great; the grief, depression, and heaviness in his head had vanished. There was a steadfast desire to live and act, and confidence and strength of mind increased a hundredfold. His mind was calm, he felt unprecedented steadiness and clarity of thought. Joseph realized that he had become the owner of an idea that had never occurred to him before.

- What had really happened to me? Was it really happening? What if I am the new Messiah on earth, who is to bring people the next prophecy, the New Testament of the Almighty? - he whispered.

Joseph went to the window and opened it wide. The fresh air touched his red-hot face. He took a deep breath and closed his eyes as he continued to enjoy the coolness. He closed the window and went to the mirror to look at himself. He didn't look quite pleasant yet: his face was still drained, a week's worth of stubble on his cheeks, black circles under his eyes from the sleeplessness and anxiety that had plagued him. But his eyes already radiated calmness, confidence, and... love. Yes, indeed! He looked at himself and saw that his eyes were full of love.

It was about eleven o'clock in the morning. Joseph quickly went to the bathroom, took a shower, shaved, cleaned himself up, and drove to work. Answering numerous greetings and questions about his well-being on the way, he walked into the office of the president of the company. From the threshold, he surprised the boss by asking him to replace him with his deputy. This step was justified by the recent general manager of the company by the fact that he needed more free time to carry out an extremely important mission, which would soon be announced publicly. Joseph's speech seemed so convincing, calm, and at the same time radiating love and respect, that it was difficult to contradict him. On the contrary, he wanted to do everything he could to help such a man in some way.

Eventually, the president did not object, but simply regretted that such a highly qualified professional was giving up a position he undoubtedly deserved. After Joseph left his office, the chief was in a state of stupor for some time, being under the spell of his now former employee.

Chapter 13

The first thing Joseph did was to sit down at his desk and write the "Divine Manifesto". The result was a short text, an appeal to all mankind.

Joseph had his own website, where he posted it in the hope that someone would respond.

It had the following text:

A MESSAGE TO MANKIND!

I, Joseph, have been chosen by the Almighty and the Supreme Ruler of the universe as a messenger to all mankind. I received this message from God through his prophets, Moses, Buddha, Jesus, and Mohammed.

Brothers and Sisters! I give you God's true message with the blessings of his former messengers. My mission is to break down the barriers created by religions between people and nations.

I tell you, people have only one Faith! It is Faith in the one true God. God, the Almighty Creator, never divided people by color or nationality. Almighty God created the stones and breathed life into them, which was the beginning of dead and living nature, which developed according to God's laws. These laws have been called the laws of nature or evolution by scientists.

Oh, people, I seek to reach your souls and open your eyes to a simple truth that is very difficult to understand and accept!

Those who have ears - hear this!

We all walk under the same God, the Creator of everything. Not understanding or even rejecting this is a great misunderstanding, that goes all the way back to antiquity.

In the beginning, the Jews were chosen by God as his people. Later each successive religion claimed that its God was the real God, not accepting the faith of others in the One Creator and thereby creating the same polytheism in the minds of believers that was common to the Gentiles. This is the greatest sin! And God has always punished and will always punish mankind as long as they believe in "different" gods. This is the greatest heresy and the greatest sin of mankind, which has not yet come to the One Creator.

God had four major agreements with mankind:

1. *The agreement with Israel through the prophet Moses.*

2. *The agreement with Buddha.*

3. *The agreement with Jesus Christ.*

4. *The agreement with Mohammed.*

The fifth agreement was made with me through the blessed prophets. People, this was done in the name of saving the world from the great sin of ethnic strife and hatred!

I am speaking to you at the threshold of another catastrophe, for I have been sent to you to prevent it! Satan wants to destroy us, to ruin us by dividing us and setting us against each other. Satan is sowing doubt in our souls about the possibility of uniting all nations and races, worshipping the One Creator who is one for all.

Remember! Dividing is a great sin, and those who divide and conquer are great sinners.

We, humans, desperately need respect and understanding, for this is the only way to prevent catastrophe and achieve peace!

People still cannot understand that our planet is a shared homeland and that peace is its spiritual harmony. The Holy Scripture says, "Enter through the narrow gate; for the gate is wide and the road is easy that leads to destruction, and there are many who go through it; for the gate is narrow and the road is narrow that leads to life, and there are few who find it.

Believers keep God's commandments, and love of others is one of them. But now I am talking to you about the relationship between nations. Here we, believers, give God the gratitude for the respect he has given us that we should have for one another. People of different faiths and religions must unite in their efforts to bring to the world the importance of inter-ethnic acceptance. It is not for nothing that the philosopher Spinoza said, "Not to laugh, not to cry, not to curse - but to understand". This is what should dominate human thinking, this is what is the key to Respect!

The Respect I preach means only one thing: Do for others what you expect for yourself. This is the only possible inter-ethnic morality that will help make humanity united and peaceful.

For thousands of years, the Almighty has chosen messengers who brought people faith in the Creator. Through it, people were imbued with wisdom and love, peace and justice, morality and goodness. Thus, gradually the Lord strengthened and expanded His strongholds among the expanding population. And now the majority of mankind believes in One God.

A time of change is coming! People, divided by religion and discord, will come to Faith in One God. For there is no other God than the one who created the universe. The Creator is the same for Jews, Christians, Muslims, Hindus, Buddhists, doubters, and atheists. After realizing this simple truth, nations must look at each other in a new way.

My brothers and sisters, if we believe in the same Creator, what can separate us? What religious barriers, traditions, and customs? What or who is more important than the Creator? Nothing and no one! God created the world order, and the highest human goal is to know God, follow him, and merge with him! This is the meaning of existence and happiness for human beings.

I am not asking you to become alike, no! I am only asking people of different religions and confessions to stop looking at each other as enemies or unbelievers, and to see each other as co-believers, i.e. as monotheists.

In the respect of one nation for another is the Faith in One God, because you believe in the same Creator. Only by believing in One God can mankind be united. Every nation is worthy of respect! There are bad people and good people, but there are no bad nations!

This is the new religion - the religion of the nations of the world! This is the Faith of the One God, these are the nations who believe in the One Almighty.

If every religion teaches its followers to respect other nations, it will contribute to their rapprochement and can guarantee peaceful coexistence on Earth.

People, at the threshold of a possible catastrophe I beseech you never to repeat the horrors of the twentieth century! For we need peace and respect on this unique planet. Our Almighty may have different names, for nations speak different languages. He may be called Jehovah, Allah, Brahman, God, but He is one Creator for all.

Get imbued with the idea of mutual respect and peaceful coexistence! Humanity is experiencing a great spiritual crisis, different religions are pitting us against each other, and people are rapidly losing faith in their bright future, and in the meaning of their important purpose. An inexorable charge of violence and fear is placed in every soul! Through the path of sin the human world has come to the brink of an abyss, it is wholly seized by an abyss that calls it to a fatal step. And I am sent to you with one purpose: to resist this mad urge!

Пришла очередь для всех тех, кто осознаёт этот кризис и считает возможным выйти из него, дабы сплотиться и начать проповедовать людям Новую Религию, основанную на Вере в Единого Бога, открывающую человечеству прекрасное будущее, где будут царить уважение и мир! Только эта Вера спасёт наших потомков от смерти и сохранит Единое Человечество.

Hear me and remember, the New Faith is ONE HUMANITY worshipping ONE GOD! This is the Faith that will lead to PEACE and RESPECT ON EARTH!

Today's society is in such a precipitous decline that it can destroy and drag down everything God has created on Earth by His greatest mercy. Humans have neither the intelligence nor the will to sever the umbilical cord that binds them to Satan. And most importantly, they have no Faith in the very possibility of their victory over the dark forces, without which the unity and brotherhood of mankind are unthinkable. And only a new Faith in One Creator, taking possession of the hearts and thoughts of all peoples, can lead to the formation of One Humanity.

I am called by our Lord to bring this Faith to the nations, as Buddha, Moses, Christ, Muhammad, and other prophets did. I am called to create an image of the One Humanity, as the Great Son of God. Without this Faith, the human community will perish.

The One God will end the division of churches and peoples, polytheism and paganism, continuous strife and enmity over territories and resources. May the One and Only Universal God become incarnate in our global unity! Globalization is God's plan, and only united humanity can bring it to a peaceful end.

I, Joseph, bring to you, people, a new Divine Manifesto, the purpose of which is One Humanity and permanent universal peace on Earth. We must take the path that leads to the end of social, political, religious and ethnic wars. This is the main goal of all mankind.

To move toward it, it is necessary to reach an understanding among nations. To achieve this understanding, I, Joseph, propose three fundamental principles of the New Faith:

1. *All of us human beings have a soul, which is a part of the Spirit of God.*

2. *All of us human beings have one home: our earth.*

3. *All of us human beings have faith in the One Almighty.*

These are the three main principles, faith in which will lead to One Humanity and peace on Earth!

The very next day Joseph's website began to receive feedback from all over the world. He barely had time to look through them as the number of responses was so great.

A couple of days later he got a call from David. He was impressed by the power and clarity of the words of the Divine Manifesto, and he decided to stand by Joseph's side and follow him to the end.

At first, Joseph was confused by this eagerness on the part of a stranger who had never seen or known him.

The next day they arranged to meet.

A young man in his thirties, with a short beard and optical glasses, arrived at the appointed time. Anticipating the standard questions, David held out his resume, as if he was getting ready to apply for a job.

The resume stated that he had been born in Memphis, Tennessee, in 1972. His father, a non-religious Jew, was a math professor at a local university and had died of a heart attack the previous year. His mother, a Jewish woman, was an elementary school teacher, now retired and living in Memphis. David was the only child in the family, graduated from Princeton University1. Currently living in Princeton, he taught in the philosophy department.

(1 One of the most prestigious universities in the United States, one of the eight Ivy League universities, and one of the nine colonial colleges founded before the American Revolution of 1775- 1783.)

- So you have decided to dedicate your life to the New Faith, which is meant to unite all mankind?

- Yes, I'm ready for that.

- What about your professional career? Are you ready to sacrifice that?

- On the contrary, I believe my profession will help me reach hearts and open people's eyes. I'm not a career person.

- What if you have to give up everything and devote yourself entirely to worship?

Would you do that?

- Yes, I would, even now! Of course, if you agree... After a pause he added:

- The only problem is my financial situation. The fact is that I live on my teacher's salary and have no other savings. If I lose my job, I'll have nothing to live on.

- Don't worry, it's solvable. I have certain financial capabilities. So you don't have to worry about that.

- In that case, I'm all yours. After thinking about it for a while, Joseph agreed:

- Well, let's try to carry out the mission the Almighty has assigned to me.

Joseph and David rented a small room in Manhattan and set it up as an office. For a generous fee, several programmers were hired to create highly professional Websites where the Divine Manifesto was posted. Now people all over the world could become fully acquainted with the postulates of the New Faith.

Joseph and David received thousands of e-mails from enthusiastic fans. Joseph became known around the world. The clergy, politicians, and businessmen began to speak of him and his teachings; there was a flood of journalists. Neophytes from all corners of the world came to hear their Messiah and get his blessing. Temples for the New Faith began to be built in many countries of Europe, Asia, Africa, and both Americas. People, imbued with Joseph's proclamation, began to call themselves monotheists and chose the meaning of their worship as the preaching of salvation to the population of the Earth by creating One Humanity believing in One God.

Of course, the world's religious institutions-churches, synagogues, and the mosque stigmatized these activities as voluntaristic and heretical, and Joseph was proclaimed an impostor who committed the sin of declaring himself a new messenger of God. The religious Muslim leaders once again reminded the world that the last prophet was the great Mohammed, and that the world had known many false messengers throughout the thirteen centuries.

But the wise Allah has always put everything in its right place. So in this case, too, Muslim theologians assured their flock.

Despite the extremely negative comments of the religious coryphaei, Joseph's teachings were becoming more and more popular by the day, and the number of his adherents was multiplying. In the age of globalization, the latest information technology and the World Wide Web have become a worthy substitute for the missionary journeys of earlier eras. Dozens of local volunteers spread the New Faith among the population. And no matter how hard the Vatican, Jerusalem, or the clergy in the East tried, they could not stop the fast-growing religious movement, which united even the most educated part of society - the intellectual elite.

These people, accustomed to analyzing and thinking independently about every phenomenon, free from the oppression of stereotypes, were more willing to believe in the Creator of Worlds and the Architect of the Universe than in holy books presented as divine revelations.

Such a turn of events was not unexpected, generally speaking. Wars and cruelty, depravity and inconstancy proved that rulers, politicians and even the United Nations were unable to cope. The modern world has reached extremes of patience with injustice and suffering that humanity has not known in millennia of development. Even after two of the most devastating wars that have taken the lives of tens of millions, we continue to see the persistent spread of evil, especially among children and young people.

"Can we ever put an end to this lawlessness and human torment?" - the monotheists asked in their sermons and confidently answered, "Yes, we can!"

As a result, people were imbued with the supreme goal of one world religion as the only possible way to harmonize life on the planet. So far, mankind has tried to change the world in different ways, but the essence of the question was different - to preserve it. The Creator will not allow thoughtless barbarians to use nuclear weapons to destroy his grand creation, the Earth. And the adherents of the New Faith will help Him in this. Those who believe in their Creator are able to stop the forces of evil and enter into the peaceful system of God, where equality and justice will prevail. Unity will save mankind.

Chapter 14

The number of followers of Joseph's teachings grew exponentially, and soon communication via the Internet was not enough. David, who took care of organizational matters, began negotiating with the authorities of New York City about a place for public speaking. After lengthy negotiations, the city fathers gave permission.

It was Joseph's first public appearance on such a scale.

The event was scheduled to take place in the city's largest stadium, located in the South Bronx and owned by the famous Yankees baseball team. However, the giant building, which had a capacity of 57,000 people, could not accommodate all those wishing to attend. Microphones were set up everywhere between the rows so that the audience had a chance to ask questions.

Joseph began with a short greeting, thanking the mayor of the city for the opportunity to communicate with people on a mass scale.

- I would like to structure my first speech in a somewhat unconventional way. I think most of those present here are familiar with my teachings, and I will not waste your time repeating truths that are already known. Therefore, I will ask you to start asking questions right away! Then we can have a productive exchange of opinions.

The first question was posed by Mr. Robinson, a "nonbeliever from New Jersey," as he introduced himself:

- I consider your teachings to be just another utopian nonsense, like Communism or any other religion that calls people through Faith to come to love and brotherhood. None of this is feasible, because human nature is fundamentally animal. Hatred and spite will always bind us together!

To this angry rebuke Joseph decided to respond with the following:

- Real Faith is not utopia. It can move mountains. Yes, we see that even within one religion there are seemingly insurmountable disagreements, even going so far as to have fellow believers kill each other. And that is terrible indeed. But notice that the conflict between different religions and even civilizations is perceived quite naturally! For example, the confrontation between Christians and Israel with the Muslim world has long been something commonplace, a matter of course! Such a reality creates a sense of hopelessness on the way to our goal. But I am convinced that Faith in One God is the only cure for sick humanity. Believing in the obvious truth, that God is one for all the people of this world, will help ease the enormous tensions that have accumulated over the centuries. The intra-religious disagreements indulged in by spiritual leaders will become marginalized and, in time, localized and subside. Peace will spread across the earth, and thus there will be fewer outbreaks of hatred and evil. As the great Zhuang Tzu said: "Hide the world in the world and there will be nowhere for it to go."

- Dear Joseph, why were all the prophets, with the exception of Buddha, of Jewish origin? After all, even Muhammad is a distant relative of the Jews. His ancestor Ishmael was the son of Abraham, the forefather of the Jews.

- It was the will of God that the Jews were to fulfill the mission that God had once given to His chosen nation, namely to bring the idea of the One God to all people. Thus, Abraham and his people believed in our Creator and told others about Him. God told me to bring to the world the good news of the coming Unity and Fraternity of those who believe in One God.

- And what do you, dear Joseph, think of Christ? Is he the Son of God or not?

- I do not question in any way the divine nature of the birth of Jesus of Nazareth. But Christ is not unique in this regard, for every person possesses a divine essence. We all have a part of God in us. The human soul is a small particle of the Creator. Jesus was the greatest example to us of how the dormant spark of the Lord should be realized. It's another matter that some may or may not realize it. But God is in all of us, and we are all in God! That is why Buddha, Mohammed and Moses are first of all the sons of God. God set these men apart from all others and made them guides of his Word. But Christ, in accordance with his will, sacrificed himself to atone for our sins. God sacrificed his Son so that people would finally come to their senses and start living according to God's commandments, which are the heritage not only of the Jewish people but also of all mankind.

Two thousand years have passed since then, and the result of that sacrifice is obvious. Through Christ, over one and a half billion people have believed in the holy commandments. Another one and a half billion Muslims accepted the One God through their messenger Mohammed. In fact, the followers of the wise Buddha, who was enlightened by the same One God, also believed in the same commandments of God. Faith in the teachings of these great mentors of mankind has not diminished over the centuries. Think about it, billions have believed them for thousands of years!

- How does your teaching differ from that of Jesus Christ?

- Now, by God's will, there is an age of integration of the human Faith, which will create a new religion of mankind. In fact, there is nothing new about it. Faith in the Universal God has always been there. It is only necessary to understand that the God in whom they believe individually belongs to all people on earth. The Creator is the same for all! We call ourselves monotheists, which means we believe in One God. We need a conscious Faith, like Buddhists believe, for example. And religions should take the best from each other: love and forgiveness from Christians, wisdom from Buddhists, knowledge and literacy from Jews, and patience and respect from Muslims.

You are all familiar with the biblical saying, "Love your neighbor as yourself". I would not dare to ask you that much. I pray and urge you to respect your neighbor's right to be yourself. God has taught us the wisest thought: Whatever you do not wish for yourself, do not wish for another. This also applies to inter-ethnic relations.

- Do you have any proof that you are not just another impostor or madman who decided to become famous? In other words, people want a miracle!

- A miracle? They will get it! The first step to the creation of the United Humanity is a fair resolution of all interethnic, interreligious, and interstate conflicts on the Earth. And it will happen very soon! Isn't it a miracle? We will show the world that our Faith is not declarative or utopian, but capable of active action. We will test it first of all in resolving ethnic disputes in a way that is fair to all conflicting parties. The world will be convinced of its power! I urge you, people, to unite under the name of our Universal Creator and understand that there is no deception in my words!

Chapter 15

By announcing his intention to reconcile the warring nations, Joseph made many people think of a better life. Long-disillusioned people who had lost confidence in authority wanted to hope!

Joseph had a clear plan of action. Too much resentment and hatred had accumulated because of the long confrontation over the disputed territories. These lands had become a deep bleeding wound in the body of the planet, and now they could not be given to any of the parties or divided between both of them. It took time for these sores to heal. A transitional period was needed. During this time, the conflict zone was to be turned into a zone:

1) demilitarized,

2) a free-economic zone.

The transition status was supposed to be for a period of about ten to fifteen years. During that time, the zone was to be directly subordinated to international societies, like the United Nations or the European Union, and was to be under the control of international security forces, like United Nations peacekeeping forces. This free economic territory would be authorized to accept all refugees from both sides who wished to return to their homeland.

A landmark event in the recognition and popularization of Joseph's teachings was the arrival of a young professor of theology at Alexandria University, Tahir Abduh, from Egypt to New York. He was named in honor of Tapahi Tahir Abduh, the great Egyptian religious scientist, jurist, and liberal reformer of the late 19th century, who dreamed of modernizing Muslim institutions and advocated the separation of politics from religious reform.

The young Tahir Abduh also advocated reform of the most orthodox Shariah provisions that prevented the adequate development of Muslims in the modern world, and he was known as a black sheep among his colleagues. When Abduh first heard about Joseph, he knew it was a sign from heaven. Leaving his work and loved ones and leaving his home, he set out for another continent. Like David, the young theologian agreed to devote himself to new teaching, for he was convinced that the New Faith was the only way to transform humanity, on the brink of mutual destruction, into a united family.

Joseph liked him from the first moment he met him. He was an intelligent, energetic young man of thirty-eight, with a small beard, slightly touched with gray. Apparently, God himself had sent to Joseph such a companion, dreaming, like his great predecessor, of the reformation of Islam.

Tahir immediately became actively involved in the work. He traveled to Muslim countries and met with religious leaders. Not many people understood him, and few accepted him, sometimes even threatening him physically.

Every time Joseph asked him not to visit dangerous regions. But Tahir merely shrugged it off, saying that sitting in New York would accomplish nothing.

One day David, entering Joseph's office, gave an official invitation to speak in Jerusalem.

- Many people in the holy city want to hear you, Joseph! I think it is very symbolic that you received your first invitation to preach publicly abroad from this holy place.

Joseph accepted the invitation with great joy and excitement. This was the first time he had been to Israel. Joseph wanted to speak at a stadium where Jews and Palestinians would be invited and where there would be simultaneous interpretation from English into Hebrew and Arabic.

At Ben-Gurion International Airport, Joseph and his friends were welcomed by the Tel Aviv city government. The meeting was very warm, and after a few hours, the guests were taken to Jerusalem, where they were to rest before the event tomorrow.

The huge Teddy Stadium, named after the former mayor, Teddy Kollek, was located in the new part of the city and was able to accommodate about 22,000 people.

A high stage with microphones was built in the middle of the soccer field. Four giant screens for simultaneous translation were installed there.

The crowd was packed to capacity, and there wasn't an inch to spare. All the space was occupied by crowds of people. It seemed as if the entire Israeli police force had arrived. The authorities feared a terrorist attack.

- God has made it so, Joseph began, that everything in the world has its turn. And King Solomon was just a genius who said: All things have their time.

Brothers and sisters, the era of the One Faith of mankind is coming! For many centuries people have been walking slowly but surely to God, to their Origin, because God is the Creator, the origin of the universe, and the universe is the offspring of the Divine Source. The time has come to a new stage of the path!

Why has God chosen our time? Because humanity is in danger! Of course, the concept of time has nothing to do with it. The danger comes from us! Mankind becomes suicidal and attempts to destroy this unique creation of God!

You can see what is going on around us. Politicians frighten people with conflicts of civilizations, which are artificially painted in religious colors. Christians are scared of Muslims. Muslims are scared of the West and Zionism. Christians and Muslims are afraid of Asians. But we, the believers in the One God, are able to prevent the coming international and inter-religious conflicts! Let me give you an example. Christians and Jews believe that Allah is the God of Muslims. But the truth is that Allah is the Arabic name for the universal God. The point is not in terms of language, but that Allah, or God, or Brahman, is one for all of us!

Suddenly someone loudly, apparently using a trumpet, shouted:

- Muslim brothers! We cannot believe what this Jew says!

Raising his hand to indicate that he had heard the remark, Joseph continued:

- Yes, I am Jewish by birth. But remember that Jesus, who preached a new faith different from the Jewish faith, was an ethnic Jew as well. And his disciples, the apostles, were Jews. But that did not stop them from playing their part.

The numerous nations who embraced the Islamic faith did not ask what the origin of Muhammad was. All are equal before the Almighty. For the Creator, all human beings are God's creatures. To you, I am not a Jew. For you, I am the harbinger of the New Faith. The Faith in the all-human God!

In fact, beginning with Abraham, the forefather of the Jewish nation, people began to believe in One Almighty God. And each new religion thought it was their Almighty, and called Him in their own language: God, Allah, Jehovah, Adenoya1, Brahman, Vishnu. This was a delusion. For the Almighty is One, no matter what He is called. He is the source of everything in the universe, and He cannot be anyone's. He belongs to all of us, to all mankind, even if individuals and nations are unaware of it. And everything belongs to Him!

(1 One of the Hebrew names for God.)

People, Jews and Muslims, you should know that you are brothers, you should know that you believe in the same God, but you still keep feuding with each other!

When you are convinced that you truly believe in One God, your enmity will be replaced by respect. The Palestinians, motivated by this faith, will stop the militants who have forgotten how to create and know only how to destroy. Then the Jews will tear down the wall between the brothers they have been building for so long!

Joseph's mesmerizing, calm voice touched the soul of everyone listening to him. People were impressed by his confidence, fearlessness, and openness. His fervent conviction was transmitted to the audience, and all those who were present began to look at old problems with renewed hope, realizing with amazement that it was possible to live with neighbors without war and terrorist attacks. These were the first such thoughts after the creation of the State of Israel, when shootings, assassinations, and "mop-ups" of shahids were an everyday occurrence. For decades, the world's most powerful countries have been trying to resolve this conflict, but the parties have been unwilling to make any concessions. And so a man of Jewish origin appeared from across the ocean and testified in the name of God that he was the new Messiah. He had not come from heaven, but had lived among humans, like the prophets before him, until the Almighty admonished him.

Someone interrupted Joseph again by shouting into the loudspeaker:

- As you know, the Jewish God punished the Jewish people severely when Israel disobeyed! What would your God do?

- In those far-off days, God acted in such a way as to reveal Himself to the Jewish people. God wanted the people to believe in Him, and He sent down God's punishment for unbelief. But with the coming of Christ, God never threatened mankind with extermination again! Humans were destroying each other themselves. Mankind punishes itself daily, for it has not yet come to the idea of a Universal, One Almighty. In reality, humanity has always been one in its diversity. The followers of my teachings will not destroy one another with such hatred, for the monotheists are people of one Faith in the One Almighty. Through me, God sends a message that the time has come for our religious unification!

Those who do not want peace on earth and try to provoke strife say that the Judeo-Christian and Islamic traditions are opposed to each other. In fact, Islam, like Christianity, originated in the depths of Judaism and came out of it. Conceptually, Christianity and Islam are based on the Old Testament, which means they are based on the Jewish Torah. It is therefore more correct to speak of a Judeo-Christian-Islamic unified tradition.

Another claim that Western civilization is the offspring - of the Greco-Roman tradition only - is also far from the truth. For example, the Arab civilization has contributed a great deal to the formation of modern Western civilization. Arabic science, medicine, music, and poetry have given mankind many new ideas and masterpieces. Even if at some point in history, Indian and Chinese civilizations developed autonomously from the West, the last centuries have seen a continuous convergence of human experience.

Therefore, it is wrong to divide the world into different, especially opposing each other civilizations. It is more correct to believe that there is a single modern civilization on Earth. And it is called the Human Civilization! One can only agree that the different nations of this global civilization are at different stages of their cultural, scientific, and technological development. The diversity of cultures is the wealth of all mankind. There is no Chinese or Japanese civilization, only Chinese or Japanese traditions and culture.

Our faith is designed to unite nations, not to sow discord. We believe in One God, who sent, through His chosen prophets, His Word of God to all people on earth. And of course, without this, without their teachings - the spiritual and moral education of mankind would not have been successful. The Monotheists preach the idea of One Humanity with a common Faith in One God. That is our goal!

Most of the people in the stadium, fascinated by Joseph's innovative ideas, listened silently and nodded their heads in agreement, not sure why they were so inspired by his speeches. It was strange to see how Israelis and Palestinians, standing in the same crowd, were beginning to look at themselves, at their neighbor, at the whole world with a different perspective.

"Why is everyone so peaceful? - Inwardly they were amazed. - Is it really possible? After all, we have been at war for so long..."

They all seemed as if they were about to embrace and forget their old grievances.

Joseph, meanwhile, continued:

- I urge the spiritual leaders of all the world's religions to start communicating with each other as closely as possible. The Almighty wants this from us! The understanding that all the believers of the world worship One God can be the beginning of the path that leads to One Humanity! The sooner modern society realizes this, the wiser, purer and nobler it will become, and above all, the more it will be saved from self-annihilation!

All nations are different, because we are all different. They are different only because one nation discovered the One and Undivided God earlier than the other, while the other is still on its way. That is God's Providence!

Once again, we want to praise the first nation that realized and believed in the One World God! God chose the Jews as pioneers with one great mission: first, to understand Him for themselves; second, to spread this knowledge to other nations.

Also. History shows us how as nations accepted the Faith in One God - with the help of the teachings of Moses, Christ, Mohammed, Buddha - they received an additional powerful passionate impulse for their spiritual and material development.

The time has come - and the Almighty desires the unity of humankind under His rule! He loves us, and we all desperately need Him!

If Christianity has been preaching love for two thousand years, then our New Faith brings respect and peace between nations. I realize it is naive to hope that any nation will love another as much as it loves itself. But it can and must respect it! They say it is one step from love to hate. But from respect to hatred, the way is very long.

Some people believe that the way to peace is through war. That is what they say: If you want peace, get ready for war. I don't believe that! Such a philosophy ultimately makes life an endless chain of wars. I believe myself and I urge you to believe that the way to harmony on earth is through the worship of mankind to One and Indivisible God!

Chapter 16

Even people who had not previously believed in God gradually began to join the New Faith. Their main motive was the preservation of humanity as humankind on Earth, peace and tranquility in the world.

The Vatican began to worry about undermining Christian foundations. The Muslim world, which until then had been immovable in matters of the canons of the Sharia and the Quran, was no longer so. For the first time in history, there were Muslims openly preaching the New Faith. And they were not alone - the process took on a mass character. The main credit for this belonged to Joseph and Tahir.

Tahir Abduh became more and more popular in the spiritual world of the East as a preacher of the New Faith. The number of his supporters was regularly increasing, and this could not but disturb the supreme clergy of Muslim countries. With the power of his faith and vitality, Tahir energized even the submissive and very conservative Mohammedans. No longer were the reform-minded solitary Muslims, always regarded as outcasts and kafirs,1 but ordinary believers were imbued with his passionate proclamations.

(1 Kafir, or qafir, from Arabic, "unbeliever," "non-believer.")

After the Jerusalem sermon, Joseph and his friends flew to New York, and the indefatigable Tahir traveled to Syria, where he was invited to speak to the followers of Islam.

The next day in the main square of Damascus, one of the oldest cities in the world, founded, according to tradition, by Adam and Eve, Tahir delivered the following speech:

- My faithful brothers! Today I wish to speak to you about the importance of dialogue, understanding and rapprochement between the Muslim world and the West.

His speech was immediately interrupted by a sharp protest:

- This talk is a waste of time! Why does the rich West need us, tens of millions of poor and destitute people? They are only interested in our natural resources!

A second voice supported him:

- We are not on the same way with the infidels. And you are an apostate! May you be damned! Burn in hell!

This is what the people in the crowd shouted in response to Tahir's words. Abduh tried to continue:

- We can learn a lot from the West...

But he was immediately contradicted with even more fervor:

- We have nothing to learn from them! Our children and wives have nothing to learn from them! Allah has left the part of the world where the Devil rules. Condoms are provided in schools, promoting... carnal pleasures between teenagers! - The fanatics kept screaming.

- Brothers, let me finish! Not everyone in the West has lost faith in God. Most ordinary people believe in the same Almighty whom you honor as well, you honorable Muslims. The Quran says, "Allah does not forbid you to be kind and fair to those who did not fight you because of your religion and did not drive you out of your dwellings. Verily Allah loves the impartial. We are not forbidden to comprehend the following ayat1 in terms of balancing the entire logic of the Quran: "Perhaps God will decide to establish friendship between you and those with whom you are hostile. For He is the Almighty, the Forgiving, the Merciful. Think about it, if we understand that dialogue is necessary and salvific, how and where to conduct it if we initially cut off all contact with non-Muslims? Not only that, Allah admonishes: "If you enter into an argument with the people of the Scriptures, conduct it in the best way possible." And one should not shy away from the conversation while trying to bring the truth to the interlocutor!

(1 An ayat is the smallest structural unit of the Quran, usually understood as "verse.")

The Quran also says, "This is Allah or God. He is one for all. The Quran says that if people adhere to the Torah and the Gospel or what is sent down to them from their Lord, they deserve the best. And next, remember? "There is no God except One God! The only difference is that each nation has its own messenger. Every nation has its own time. Every time has its own Scripture! And only Satan sows discord among people."

Brothers, don't be among those who have divided the Faith in One God!

Each subsequent Scripture confirms the previous one. Allah gave you the Law of Faith bequeathed to Noah, Abraham, Moses, Jesus, and Mohammed. Keep the Faith right, that is, one and only, and do not divide yourselves in it!

Abduh's last words were met with less fierce opposition:

- You are right. Allah gave the children of Israel the Scripture and the authority and gave his preference. But they turned from the way of God and sowed disorder among the people!

- Those who have ears to hear, hear! We don't need enmity and hatred now; the world is already choked with blood! Cruelty and immorality appear in our lives from lack of knowledge and little wisdom, from not seeing the consequences of one's immoral actions. To be wise is to be good, the Buddha teaches.

It is written in the Quran that the faithful acknowledge the scriptures previously sent down by Allah. Remember, Muslims, God's second commandment, "Do not make yourself an idol". So, maturity is a clear understanding that you must be yourself and not someone else's copy. Don't imitate anyone, be natural! Imitation comes from the outside, someone gives you an ideal, and you follow it blindly.

God will not ask you why you did not become Muhammad, may the Almighty bless and keep him! He will ask why you did not become you. It doesn't matter who you are! What is important is what you will appear as before God's Gate! The crowd gradually calmed down and began to listen carefully to the preacher's words.

- Brothers, hear me! I am sure that the West and we have a lot to learn from each other. For example, we, Muslims, pride ourselves on the fact that the bonds of our brotherhood are stronger than family bonds, proud of our kindness and respect for our elders, parents and children. When I say "learn from the West," I am aware that such concepts as democracy, civil society and human rights seem foreign and distant to us. But that is not what we are talking about now.

We have to learn to rely only on ourselves! Every Muslim must learn to act on his own, without relying on his parents, his boss, the Shah, the Sheikh, or the West. He must believe in God and in himself!

When people become hardworking and law-abiding, when they honor family, wife and children above all else, then they can strengthen any country! These simple principles of life once helped the Puritans create nations like Germany, England, and the United States. These countries are powerful, progressive, and at the same time attractive to the people of the world. In contrast, the social aggression exhibited by many young Muslims widens the gap between wishful thinking and reality. I'm telling you: to stop the strife, you need to stick to the simple rules of life that I said earlier.

I know that you, young and strong people, want good jobs, wealth, and security for your families, want a good life for yourselves and your loved ones! I understand why you resent my urging you to visit libraries to learn about the profound knowledge that mankind has accumulated over the millennia. On an empty stomach, it is really difficult to listen to the ornate thoughts of the sages. I believe that it is much easier to take a gun and kill or rob, thereby carrying out a false "justice" that changes nothing. I understand how hard it is to turn things around! But that's the thing, without peaceful work, without peaceful effort, nothing will work out for us. Acquiring knowledge, and working hard, is much harder than destroying someone or even yourself. Changing one's principles in life is very difficult, but necessary! And education and informational support can play a tremendous role in this. The time has come for talented educators, organizers, and journalists. That is the power!

If a nation has enough of these people at its disposal, it already represents a certain power and can influence the rest of the world by offering it its religion, its traditions, its national "self" and their view of controversial issues.

Unfortunately, in this field, we, Muslims, have a very sad statistic. In the last hundred years, only three out of one and a half billion members of this faith on earth have won the Nobel Prize. There are only about 500 universities in 57 Muslim countries. By comparison, there are 5,758 universities in the United States and 8,407 in India. The average literacy rate in the Muslim world is less than forty percent, compared with ninety percent for Christians. In Muslim countries only fifty percent of the population finish secondary school and two percent graduate from universities; in Christian countries, these figures are ninety-eight percent and forty percent respectively. For Muslims there are only two hundred and thirty scientists with different professions for every one million people; in the United States alone there are, come to think of it, five thousand!

Thus, in the Muslim world, there is an urgent need for societal and state modernization without losing one's identity. Fear of inept reforms leads the Muslim world to reject innovation, believing that

Muslim self-determination might suffer. They are not ready to sacrifice their centuries-old traditions to the processes of globalization and modernization they do not understand.

My fellow Muslims! I, Abduh Tahir, a disciple of the last Messiah on earth, the honorable Joseph, declare that he has come to bring us God's message! Now Muslims have an important task: not to keep fighting against foreigners, sacrificing their young lives for the Heavenly Paradise, but to look at the world and other nations with new horizons. You should not see them as enemies, but as your respected neighbors, united by Faith in the One and Only Almighty, who is the One to us all!

Chapter 17

After Joseph's return from Jerusalem to New York, he was cursed and threatened by the high and mighty of the world. The Vatican officially declared him a heretic spreading God-impeding heresy, and Islamic leaders accused him of imposture. Tahir was also convicted to death by the fanatics of Islam. He was accused of having sold his soul to Zionists and American imperialism, of having broken the laws of Sharia, of urging the faithful to respect and understand infidels who only dream of destroying all Muslims or exploiting their lands in their own interests.

All these attacks demanded a wise response, preferably with an appeal to the intellectual elite of the United States. David, a talented organizer, negotiated permission for a speech at the famous Columbia University in northwestern Manhattan. The institution was founded in 1754 as King's College, having received a charter from King George II of England. Between 1901 and 2000, 78 scientists from the famous university won the Nobel Prize.

In front of the Philosophy Department building, where Joseph's speech was to be delivered, stood one of the copies of Auguste Rodin's famous sculpture "The Thinker," the embodiment of a painfully nascent human thought.

The huge conference hall was full of people who wanted to hear the preacher. Many guests from other states and countries arrived as well.

As Joseph approached the pulpit, the crowd fell silent.

- Brothers and Sisters! - he addressed them. - The authorities, the military leadership, and the clergy benefit from keeping the present situation in the world unchanged. They suggest to people that life on earth is just a short and sinful moment, which means that we, the temporal guests in it, must suffer humiliation, poverty, and injustice. After death, however, we are promised eternal happiness in paradise. But, in order to get there, we have to do what we are told, we have to live as they decide for us, that is, we have to hate and kill those who will be pointed at by their pointing finger. And only then - hear me, only then! - by sacrificing our only lives for their ideas, we will, according to their promises, go to heaven!

And these sacrifices are demanded of us by those who at this time are living on sinful earth as in Paradise! They have long ago established an earthly paradise for themselves, and would not trade it for a phantom heavenly kingdom, promised after death!

God sacrificed his son, Jesus Christ, to atone for our sins, including the worst. For what? So that we would finally stop hating and killing each other! Imagine, just for a moment, that this has happened. What would our planet be like, where there would be peace, tranquility and understanding? Would you recognize it? That would be the Heavenly Paradise where everybody wants to go - but on Earth. Thus, God Himself, through the sacrifice of Christ, wished to create an Earthly Paradise for all people, not just for those with power!

So, human beings, created by God, are worthy to live their lives in the conditions of the earthly Paradise and then to die and go to the Paradise in Heaven. This is the plan of God, the victory of humanity over the Devil, who still holds sway over the souls of the majority, is based on this! We, humans, need to cast aside egoism and pride, the chief of Satan's inventions, from which arises all evil and hatred.

We, followers of monotheism, ask the authorities and the clergy: don't ordinary people deserve to live on Earth as they do in their Earthly Paradise? At least without wars and in peace, not as victims of their interests.

If the authorities want to remain the authorities, they must try to pacify any military and national conflicts, they must stand up for peace on a planetary scale. The clergy should support them by teaching people that humanity is one family that believes in One God. And there is no difference between a Christian, a Mohammedan, a Jew, or a Buddhist, because they are all God's creatures, and all truly love the One Almighty.

Over the past fifty-five years, mankind has been smart enough not to start a global world war. And there are good reasons for this. The main reason is fear, because we all share the same Earth. That is why all political intrigue is concentrated on local, interethnic conflicts. The feelings of international hatred can be easily manipulated from above, because for centuries, nations have accumulated enough claims to each other. There is no small amount of blame to be attributed to the clever, so-called "advocates for the people," who masterfully foment national hatred. I am not even mentioning those in power; enough has already been said about them. Look at what is going on in the former Soviet Union and former Yugoslavia, in the Middle East and Africa! Everywhere inter-ethnic conflicts are smoldering or flaring up, poisoning existence and inflaming feelings of hatred towards each other.

We, monotheists, do not want that! We strive to turn enmity and hatred into respect and understanding. We respect all religions. And let the Christian still believe in love for neighbor. May the Muslim be convinced that all people will become faithful. May the Jew continue to zealously follow his Laws. May the Buddhist yearn for contact with the macrocosm, and renounce material possessions. Let it be! But to all this, we shall add mutual respect and acceptance, which will be promoted by Faith in the One Almighty for all of us.

So, respect and peace to you, nations of the earth, for that is what God wants from people right now! This is the message His venerable prophets conveyed to me. The search for world harmony is the One Humanity worshipping the One Creator God!

The enlightenment of the 18th and 19th centuries set itself against God, and people's faith began to weaken. But now, in the age of the highest rise of scientific thought and innovative technology, they once again remembered their Creator. And this is symbolic. Only He, not the achievements of science, can curb hatred and evil.

One of the main tasks of the world's religions is to educate followers in behavior that is based on identifying them with their neighbors. Because one cannot do to another anything one does not want done to himself. Our New Faith is based on this fundamental principle, because it is the only one that should be the basis of international relations. Even though we are far from this model today, we need to recognize this commandment of God for the survival of the human species. It is necessary to apply all the strength of our Faith, all the power of our conviction to implement this rule of the community, without which it becomes simply dangerous to exist.

So, I repeat to you, salvation is in Faith! Belief in God has created common conceptions of Good and Evil that have been inherited over generations. Faith has shaped the ethics that govern a society without legal laws. Law follows moral action, and God's punishment is always stricter than human judgment.

I believe the New Faith will help solve the conflicts that murdered millions of people who were neighbors, friends and relatives for decades. It is only by recognizing that we are not divided by language, color, religion, tradition, or culture that we can come to faith in the One Almighty. It is this Faith that has made us all so different and yet so much the same. This is the case when cause and effect work together, contrary to human logic. So say YES to the one God! Say NO to blood and war!

At the end of Joseph's speech, he was bombarded with questions.

- You claim to have communicated with the Lord God Himself. Tell me, what does he look like?

- I have not seen or communicated with God. The prophets, God's messengers on earth, appeared before me. They spoke to me and blessed me with the New Faith of One Humanity in One God. Actually, all people believe in One God, but the ways to him are different.

- Do you really allow the possibility of uniting religions into One Faith?

- It is not a matter of one day, I understand, but it is possible and necessary to talk about it. Especially since this question has been discussed for hundreds of years. Religions such as Hinduism and Bahaism preach the idea that all religions actually honor one God, just under different names.

Three and a half billion believers adhere to the canons of Christianity, Islam, and Judaism. All three of these religions have been connected by unbreakable divine threads ever since the Almighty appeared to Abraham, the forefather of the Jewish people.

About two billion people practice Hinduism, Buddhism, Sikhism, Shintoism, and other Eastern spiritual teachings. They believe that there is one Creator God of the universe.

Finally, six hundred to seven hundred million people identify themselves as non-believers. They consider themselves educated, modern, with a critical mind and independent thinking. But their belief in intelligence, unfortunately, does not help to solve world conflicts and eradicate hatred between nations. Their efforts are aimed at the development of scientific and technological progress, their achievements increase the area of human comfort, but in doing so they unwittingly impose a consumerist philosophy. Lust for luxury, greed and inequality divide people and make them forget their God-given moral values. This is happening all over the world.

I urge people to turn their eyes to Faith in the One God, the Creator. This faith will not hinder, but on the contrary, will help scientific and technological research and the multiplication of material wealth.

Einstein said that science without religion is lame and religion without science is blind. The purpose of science is to establish general rules governing the relationship of objects and events in space and time. It is clear that the knowledge of what is, does not lead to the discovery of what should be. To clarify, knowledge of truth itself is a positive fact, but it is too little to serve as a guide, since there is no justification for the value of striving to know the truth. Consequently, we face the limitations of a purely rational conception of our existence. The intellect reveals to us the relationship between means and ends, but reason alone cannot clarify the meaning of ultimate, fundamental ends. Identifying these ends and making them the basis of people's emotional lives is precisely the most important function of religion.

Aren't we not children of the same Father? Are we condemned to be the victims of each other because of our own petty passions and inherited customs? Is nothing around us worth preserving? Are we not, united, called to do all in our power to eliminate the danger that threatens all alike?

God gave the world morality and taught people to treat one another with respect, for this is the only way to stop mutual annihilation. I suppose those people who think they are the masters of the earth, but forget God, also have a stake in this.

- You blame the clergy and church for hypocrisy, deceit, and other sins. But aren't you yourself just another religious profanation, leading people away from the real scriptures and traditional faith?

- You know, I sincerely believe that all religions call their followers to love. All religions are imbued with spirit and morality. They are pure! But unfortunately, people who consider themselves to be spiritual fathers and the church leadership have done and continue to do things that do not please God for thousands of years. I will not argue about it for a long time, I will simply give one example.

Why did the emperor Constantine and the Council in the year 321 after the Nativity of Christ have to change the day of worship officially for the Christians from Saturday to Sunday? After all, Jesus worshiped God on Saturday. The answer is that in order to be different, to be different from the Jews. That is, the Church itself chose to do this bypassing God and Christ. But the Church cannot change God's Word. Saturday is God's day. God rested on Saturday, and Saturday is mentioned in the fourth of His Ten Commandments. So why do

Christians follow only nine of them and deny one? When the Church or authority corrects the Holy Scriptures given by God through the prophets, they are committing a great sin!

- How do you feel about Islam?

- I deeply respect all religions, including Islam, which preaches the worship of One and Undivided God and, together with other religions, defends social justice, moral values, peace, and freedom for all people. The Quran does not call for the spread of Islam by the sword and the destruction of non-believers. We are allowed to use weapons only in defense.

- How do you feel about the claims of Islamic fanatics that they are not murderers? Do you think they are defending their Muslim values against the expansion of a depraved and insatiable West?

- Many people get cause and effect confused. Look at the United States. America was founded by religious people for whom faith in God was a fundamental principle of not only personal but also political life.

Unfortunately, in the last thirty or forty years, the West has increasingly turned away from God into a realm of liberal freedoms, showing disrespect for religious, moral, and cultural values. For a believer, whether a Muslim, a Jew, a Christian, or a Buddhist, this kind of freedom is evil.

The Muslim world is less flexible and more intransigent. And economic backwardness and poverty in many Muslim countries provide fertile ground for envy and hatred of the West, which is easy to blame for one's own troubles.

In any normal society goodness, courage, honesty, absence of selfishness, intelligence, industriousness and responsibility are honored, while such qualities as cowardice, dishonesty, selfishness, stupidity and laziness are regarded as negative. Notice, regardless of ethnicity and religion!

My point is that most of the values attributed to the West are values acquired by all mankind over many thousands of years of history.

At a later stage of development-I mean the last three hundred years-Europeans and Americans managed to become the main bearers of these universal values and, thanks to them, to achieve dizzying economic, scientific and technological progress. Later, some Far Eastern Asian countries were able to follow this path.

Therefore, it would be more correct to call the so-called "Western values" universal values, except for freedom and democracy. They are equally good for all normal people who want happiness for themselves and their children.

I appeal to Muslims not to turn away from these values, but to absorb them! Especially since they already have them, and it is only necessary to develop them in themselves. And I call the West to remember the moral and religious traditions of its forefathers-founders!

- Do you really intend to create a single world religion and a single world clergy? Doesn't this idea seem absurd to you?

- Whoever believes, he knows that faith and spirituality have no boundaries. Unity is the last chance to stop the bloody march of evil that is dragging mankind into the abyss. I believe that the world's religions have more in common than they have differences. And I am convinced of the possibility of their rapprochement on this basis.

Humanity is divided, yes. And when the whole begins to divide, there are grudges, envy, hatred, fights and murders. Who are our judges?

Dividing is always unfair to one side. But the idea of shared values will lead to compromise, the domination of good feelings, the development of common interests, and, as a result, peace.

Understand, the core essence of the human being is the same for everyone-it is divine! It's just that each religion diversifies it with ethical and ethnic features.

Turn your senses away from the terrible heresy of separation! God is one, but different religions personify Him in different ways, such as the Creator God, the God of the universe, the World Mind who created the universal order, the strict God, the merciful God, the discerning and all-seeing Allah.

Open your eyes and listen to my words! After all, all this is just a variety of names of the One Almighty!

- Are not too many Jews among the prophets? You too, honorable Joseph, have counted yourself among them...

- I have answered this question more than once. I will repeat only one thing: everything is the will of the Almighty. God chose the Jews. They were the only people who could bear the burdens of their difficult history and at the same time maintain a great faith in the One God.

- According to the Old Testament, the Hebrew God is strict and even angry.

What do you say to that?

- That is utter ignorance! We believe in God, and we don't know whether he is fair, good, or cruel. God is on the other side of good and evil! Everything else is human judgment. God is the Creator. He created all living and non-living things in our universe. God punished the Jews only when they broke his commandments and turned away from the Faith, but always protected them when they were obedient. Without God's command, the Jews, this small nation, would have been destroyed by the many giant nations among which they existed. But the Jewish ethnos not only survived, but also maintained its high status. This is God's sign.

- What kind of God do you believe in: a transcendent God or a personified God?

- God cannot be described in human terms. However, a human being describes him, he gets nowhere. God is everything and everything is God.

To me, God is transcendent, in the sense that he is the source of everything and one for all religions and all humanity. At the same time, at the level of a microcosm, each of us is a part of the Universe, or Nature, and therefore a part of God. So, the blood cell in your artery is a particle of you. A particle of God is the human soul. And the highest purpose of humans is to serve the One Creator.

- What religion did you belong to in your past life?

- I didn't have a generally accepted attitude toward faith. For me, the concepts of God and religion are in different hypostases. God is the Creator of the universe, He is one for all mankind and is indivisible. And this is a great truth. Well, religion is something that people themselves have created. Religion is a reflection of the soul and character of a people. They look in that mirror and see their reflection--the religion they worship.

Human history shows us that religions, unfortunately, contribute to the division of humanity. Religious co-believers form its larger subdivisions, which include ethnic groups. Incidentally, only a few ethnic groups in the world have created world religions.

The Jewish ethnos gave birth to Judaism, the Western Roman ethnos to Catholicism, the Byzantine ethnos, also Greek, to Orthodoxy, the German ethnos to Protestantism, the Indian to Hinduism, Confucianism, Buddhism and Sikhism, the Arabic to Islam.

And then, by peaceful or violent means, these peoples spread their teachings among the other ethnic groups.

- I am a biologist and do not believe in the Creator of the universe. I only believe in evolution. What do you have to say against evolution?

- I sincerely regret, for you are deluded. It seems to me that the reason is that in your soul the divine spark has not yet flashed, which would help you to discern in the darkness of your soul the light that shows you the right way, the way to our God-the Creator.

Einstein, too, was a scientist and accepted the impossibility of an uncreated universe. This conclusion, the result of his work on the theory of relativity, led him to conclude that the universe had a BEGINNING and therefore a Creator.

Atheists believe that science explains everything, and if it cannot answer now, it will in the future. In fact, the scientific view of the origin of the universe is no different from the religious view: the universe arose in one moment, as a result of the Big Bang. The explosion was not accidental and was very precisely calculated, which allowed the universe not to disperse and not to shrink into a point. The Universe arose without any initial prerequisites, out of nothing and thanks to the action of the Superpower, to which all the forces of nature are subject. For a religious interpretation of this phenomenon, it is enough to replace the word "Superpower" with "God. Superpower established all the laws of macro- and microcosm - physical, chemical and biological. And if there are laws in nature - and this is a scientific fact - then there is also a Lawgiver.

This idea is confirmed by the amazing properties of nature: harmony, reproduction, regularity, expediency, symmetry and perfection. A single seed contains the entire genetic structure of a plant, and the most complex structure of organs of a multicellular living being, such as an eye or a heart (valve opens, valve closes), cannot be explained by any coincidence or evolution. Without the Creator, it is impossible to imagine not only the work of individual organs, but also the appearance of the entire plant and animal world, and especially humans talking and thinking, feeling and compassionate, ready for self-restraint or self-sacrifice.

Let me draw a little parallel. For example, there is a mountain that has been standing for centuries with a lot of metal in its depths. Can we expect that over the centuries a railroad car will arise from it? Certainly not! It requires a human being to do it. In other words, one needs a Creator, a Maker, and human beings, in this case, are his projection.

There is a legend on this subject associated with the great scientist Isaac Newton. In his well-equipped laboratory, another scientist, a follower of the evolutionary development of nature, once entered. The guest was very interested in the origin of the glittering balls. Newton replied, "These spheres came from nowhere. They were like that, they came out on their own over many centuries. No one made them." - "No way!" - said the guest. Newton objected, "Why can't it be? You don't believe that for everything there must be a creator."

Let's also look at our Earth and life on it. After all, it is a work of genius by a genius Creator! Life would simply not have been possible without certain conditions or subtle mechanisms that only revealed their secrets in the twentieth century. First, the location of our planet in the solar system and the Milky Way galaxy, the orbit of the Earth, the inclination of its axis, the speed of its rotation, and its satellite, the Moon. Second, the magnetic field and atmosphere, are a kind of double armor. Third, the abundance of water. And finally, fourth, the natural cycles that regenerate and purify the biosphere. Did all this come about by blind chance? Or is the possibility of an ingenious design more obvious?

All of the features of the Earth that I have listed testify to the wisdom of the Demiurge.

As the evolutionary physicist Paul Davies once said, "even atheist scientists are filled with awe at the scale, grandeur, harmony, intricacy, and extraordinary elegance of the universe. I ask again, could such an ingenious construction have arisen by itself, by chance? Or is it the hand of the Creator?

You, as a scientist, would probably agree with me: no two people in the world are alike, but the underlying human essence is the same. And it is divine in the sense that it contains God's spark. Each person can build a bridge between himself and God, walk toward Him throughout his life and merge with His light. Such individual "building" will be the basis for the unity of humankind. In concluding my response, I would like to recall the words of the great theologian and philosopher Francis Bacon:

"Atheism is thin ice on which one man will walk and a whole people will fall into the abyss."

- When you think of the Almighty, what do you usually ask for yourself?

- I don't ask, I just hope I'm doing what he approves. By the mere fact that people try to become aware of the One God, they become more tolerant and humane. Believers purify their thoughts, and this enables them to avoid violence and unrighteous acts. Is this not enough? Isn't that what people should strive for?

Chapter 18

Joseph's speech at Columbia University caused a sensation. The thousands of intellectuals, interested in his peculiar thinking, decided to take his side.

A few days later David's office received a phone call from a man who introduced himself as Michael. He said he was speaking on behalf of a group of people who were the heads of major corporations. "We are interested in your teachings and want to meet to establish a mutually beneficial relationship," he offered in conclusion.

David promised to talk to Joseph and get back to him. His phenomenal intuition told him that getting to know influential people would be invaluable. Wasting no time, he told Joseph about the call.

- Seeking contact with us? Why?

- They want to offer help and cooperation.

- What do they want in return?

- They assured me that our interests are the same.

- But we have no interests! We only bring people faith in the One Creator.

- I'm sorry, I misspoke... These people are in favor of integration.

And I feel that contacting them will help our cause.

- David, I trust you as myself.

- Then put it all on my shoulders. I'll contact them and work out the details.

- David, when was the last time you spoke to Tahir?

- Yesterday. He was preparing for a conference in Alexandria.

Tahir had invited famous theologians, scholars and anyone who cared about Muslims and their relationship to the world. Thanks to his tireless energy and enthusiasm, the event took place despite protests from radical Islamists. Many renowned theologians addressed the large audience with their fiery speeches.

- The Islamic world needs modernization - that is the main task! - Tahir Abduh spoke ardently from the pulpit. - Not Westernization, but modernization, as is happening in Turkey and East Asian countries, where different religions and cultures coexist with renewal.

Our reformation is hampered by many traditional Islamic attitudes: education, the status of women, criticism of political freedoms, and the intertwining of state, religion, and society. These barriers once existed in both Judaism and Christianity, but were overcome after a long struggle.

Unfortunately, the synthesis of religion and politics is at the core of the Islamic tradition. But the state and the mosque are not compatible!

Look what happened in Iran after radicals combined political power and religion! A country's constitutional norms must override religious identity. Trouble begins when a citizen considers the political culture imposed by Sharia to be superior to the political culture of the state.

I support a complete separation of the state from religion! My main concern in this segment is the separation of faith and politics in the Islamic world. A renaissance of the Islamic world can begin with this!

It is not necessary to resist renewal, it is necessary to look for approaches to it! In any case, it is better than calling to fight and defeat the West. The example of Turkey, China and Japan shows how they have embraced Western institutions while retaining the faith and core of their own culture. This is what is important!

Nowhere in the Quran does it say that war means armed confrontation. In fact, the Almighty is referring to spiritual combat. The Prophet Muhammad (peace be upon him) - made a stake on peaceful expansion. Radicals, on the other hand, look for calls in the Quran to fight the infidels, deliberately distorting and misinterpreting its words. They deceive our children with skillful propaganda, guaranteeing a paradisiacal afterlife and material security for the family left without a breadwinner. Genuine jihad is a struggle you wage in your soul, with yourself, to become a faithful Muslim, and not at all on the battlefield!

We have a lot to agree on with the West! And the main thing is the connection of Islam with Judaism and Christianity. We are all children of Adam and Abraham. We all worship the same God! And we all believe that our One God guides us through life.

At this point one of Tahir's opponents raised his hand to indicate that he wanted to ask a question. Abduh nodded respectfully.

- We, righteous Muslims, see what is happening to the West. It has gone too far in its irrepressible and insatiable appetite for profit, losing its religious and ethical dimension. Do these people, turned into soulless functionaries, heartless sensualists, these wretches, really think they have reached an unconquered stage of human development...?

- Yes, I understand your deep-seated anger very well. Human suffering and hatred... They have very deep historical roots. The Islamic states, once at the head of civilization, have lagged behind politically, economically and culturally. And not only in comparison with the

West, but also with the countries of the Far East and Russia. Former greatness breeds envy and spite. Yes, as bitter as it is, we should look first and foremost at ourselves, and not blame the more developed countries.

The East has its own perception of negative reality. We only accept the reality in which we live, even if it is unacceptable. What matters most is that it is OUR reality, even if it is anti-human.

The West, on the contrary, is always trying to change things, to make them better, to make them more human. This is our main difference. Once again, the Jewish, Islamic, and Christian ideas of One God are identical, because we are talking about the same Creator of the universe. However, different mentalities and different translations of the same word into different languages have led to disagreements and misunderstandings.

We, Muslims, have a habit of accepting life as it is with doom. The belief in fatalism, passive obedience, political impotence, lack of choice and the right to an opinion are what hinder our development. And if someone decides to protest, to fight for their terms, they will be condemned by their own peers: why are you doing all this, and what makes you do it?

Only when every Muslim accepts responsibility for at least his own life will there be an awakening. For now, our eyes are closed, but we are ready to wake up! Waking up means coming back to ourselves, becoming a creator, a part of the Creator!

Many generations of Muslims have been brought up in a spirit of hatred of the West and its values. But we are forced to accept the political system that will help us climb out of poverty and live life to the fullest. History has shown that all the systems the East has created over the millennia have failed. So we should try to adapt to the Western model, because humanity has not yet invented anything better. And believe me, it will by no means harm our Islamic sanctuaries!

Another participant asked to speak out:

- We have our own values, so we don't need Western values! Nor do we need muscularized women and feminized men. The West is rapidly losing the importance of the traditional family, which is no longer able to fulfill one of its most important functions: childbearing and education. And the sub-product that is being offered instead, called "civil marriage," is, for us, Muslims, a form of prostitution.

And same-sex relationships - is that a God-pleasing thing to do? May Allah forgive me for saying this! You are right to say that there was a time when Muslims lived in prosperous caliphates, where science, philosophy, and poetry flourished, while Europe was stuck in medieval obscurantism. But you are actually calling for the liberalisation of Islam, and that is not allowed! For Islam is now the only religion in the world that is pure before God. Look at the Christian world - homosexuality, lesbianism, pedophilia among clergymen have become commonplace. But Islam is a religion of strict monotheism, a religion that recognizes all the prophets from Adam and Ibrahim (Abraham) to Jesus and Mohammed. It is a religion that knows no borders, races, cultures, or languages. A religion that deduces human virtue not from genetic factors, but from a degree of obedience to God.

In confirmation of my thoughts, I want to quote the words of the prophet Muhammad: " Oh people! Indeed, you have one Lord, and you have one Father. You are all descendants of Adam, and Adam was created from clay. And there is no advantage for an Arab over a non-Arab, for a white person over a black person, except in the fear of God.

- Honorable Anwer, I agree with what you say. Nothing in the world is perfect, either in the West or in the East. I agree that the modern West is catastrophically losing its best religious and ethical values, which once enabled it to achieve great things. I can't accept a lot of what's going on there, and neither can you. But that's not what I want to talk to you about.

One of the founders of Protestantism, Jean Calvin, remarked, "God helps those who help themselves." He taught that professional activity is a task assigned by God to human beings. It is by deeds that we best please and glorify the Almighty. God helps us by sustaining our inner energy so that we can work and create.

We must learn to talk less and do more! Remember the commandment of silence, the biblical threat for every useless word. Remember the sin of idle talk!

Another, even more grievous sin, is wasting time. Those who waste time neglect the salvation of their souls. Human life is extremely short and precious and should be used only for the fulfillment of the mission that is intended for everyone. Wasting time on entertainment, talking, luxury, and even sleeping more than the required six to eight hours is completely unacceptable from the point of view of morality. Time is infinitely precious, for every hour lost, that is, not well spent, is taken from God, not devoted to the increase of His glory. Work, given to us from above, is the purpose of all human life.

Calvin argued that faithfulness to occupation was imposed on people as a punishment for sin. Occupation is a way of showing love to others. The only way to know oneself is not by observing oneself, but by doing. Actions speak for you, and they immediately reveal your worth.

This is what I mean when I talk about basic Western values. The Protestant Calvinists saw in TRUST their duty to God. It is the central life and ethical pivot upon which the West has risen.

So, what is my point? That we can and should learn from each other! We must adopt all that is wise and useful which would help us all to be better than we are, which would reduce human suffering, hatred, mutual destruction and poverty on earth.

In order to bring peace to the world, common ground must be found between the different religions. And the most important of these is Faith in One God.

Our world today, in spite of everything, is more perfect than ever before and is more disposed to create One Humanity believing in One God.

Chapter 19

The next day, at noon, there was a car waiting in front of David's office. When he approached the black car, the driver, a middle-aged man in a black suit, politely opened the back door and gestured for him to have a seat. David found himself in the spacious interior of the limousine, equipped like offices for business meetings.

They left the business part of Manhattan and headed in the direction of the area where the richest people in the world live, on Fifth Avenue, right in front of Central Park. Soon the car stopped in front of one of the luxurious condominiums with a conservatory on the roof of a four-story building.

A well-dressed and buffeted doorman opened the front door for them. Then he spoke to someone on the phone, and soon a young man, also dressed in a uniform, appeared and politely asked David to follow him.

How many times in his life had the professor walked down Fifth Avenue along Central Park, looking at the houses across the street, where behind every glass door stood a genteel doorman, almost in gilded livery! And never, not even in his thoughts, could he have imagined that the day would come when he crossed the threshold of one of these buildings.

The door was opened by a middle-aged man who introduced himself as Michael. He was short, stocky, and had sly, squinting, and constantly running eyes. The landlord gestured for his guest to come in. They walked through a huge room and found themselves in a small cozy office.

Michael offered David a drink, but he refused, and then the new acquaintance began to talk.

- We, that is, representatives of big business, are interested in your new religious movement and are ready to financially support and promote you at the highest levels. I think you, a person who deals with organizational matters, should not be indifferent to my proposal...

- You are well informed.

- That's my job. Once again, I emphasize that you and I can work together productively.

- What kind of assistance do you offer?

- For example, the provision of a solid headquarters in midtown Manhattan to replace the mini-office you're currently cooped up in. It would be more prestigious for a movement that's become internationally renowned. Then, your... uh... - Michael hesitated, not knowing what to call Joseph, but after a moment he realized, his spiritual master has big plans for the resolution of ethnic conflicts. I don't really know how that would work, but we'd like to support you.

- Until now, I have been convinced that it is more beneficial for those in power to divide and conquer than to reconcile.

- The fact is that the topics you address in your speeches are more about the government than they are about us, the people in business. We are not politicians, we are representatives of the business world. Our interests are related to globalization. Big business has long gone beyond national borders, it is too narrow in terms of national borders, and any entrepreneurship, especially corporate and transnational, requires a continuous increase in profits and the search for new markets and resources. Sometimes inter-ethnic conflicts get in the way of our goals. And even if these disputes are local on a global scale, they still affect vast regions, because geopolitical tensions are concentrated there and the interests of five or six countries collide. As you can see, I am quite frank with you. We think you are serious people, because your proclamations do truly amazing things!

I mean the way people from all over the world are joining you and believing the preaching of the Honorable Joseph. That's pretty much it. We are ready to cooperate with you.

- Is it true that multinational corporations have been given veto power over the legislation of any country?

- Well, that's an obvious exaggeration, answered Michael modestly. Promising to talk to Joseph and call him in a couple of days, David decided for himself that there was nothing wrong with enlisting the help of money moguls, even if it contradicted Joseph's moral principles. After all, he, David, was in charge of organizational matters, and with this unexpected suggestion, many problems could be solved.

A couple of weeks later, the assistant surprised Joseph by announcing that he had found a great place to relocate their headquarters. After all, the flock of monotheists was growing by the day, and the solid clerical movement had no choice but to squeeze into the cramped old office.

When David showed a picture of the building chosen for the new office, Joseph looked intently at his associate and inquired:

- Aren't you in touch with the moneybags?

- Any charity in God's way can be gratefully received.

- Look, David, we must do God's work with clean hands!

- Don't worry, Joseph, I'll take care of it, the friend said with conviction, looking him openly in the eye.

Chapter 20

That evening David literally burst into the office and stood there frozen.

As he turned around in his chair, Joseph saw his pale and distraught face, and immediately sensed that something was wrong. Something irreparable had happened.

He got up from the chair and came closer. David took off his glasses with one hand and rubbed his eyes with the other.

- What has happened? - Joseph asked quietly.

- Tahir...

From Alexandria, Tahir flew to Lebanon. His friends and followers in Beirut had obtained permission from the city authorities to speak in the central square of Beirut, called the Star because of the little streets radiating out from it in all directions.

Tahir's Beirut speech was his last. After the speech, he and his group got into a car and it exploded as soon as the driver started the engine.

Joseph, who had for some time been anxiously monitoring his friend's tumultuous activities and was very worried about his life, was shocked by the tragedy that had occurred. He had literally lost a brother and a devoted New Faith believer. And for the first time, he faced a real threat to himself and his movement, because one of his best followers had been killed.

Joseph flew urgently to Alexandria, where Tahir had been born and raised and where a memorial ceremony was to take place. The monotheists from many countries came to bid farewell to the preacher who had died for his faith in the One God.

Tahir was buried in the famous Hadra Memorial Military Cemetery, located in the eastern part of the city, not far from Alexandria University, where Abduh was teaching and working. Most of the soldiers who died in World War I and World War II were buried here. Some honorable civilians also found their last resting place here.

At the memorial service, Joseph spoke to all those assembled:

- Now I see that there are so many of us who are like-minded! Every day I am convinced that we are on the right path, because we were blessed on this path by our venerable prophets, who did the will of the Almighty. May there be peace on earth! The great son of the Egyptian people, Tahir Abduh, sacrificed his life for this purpose!

In his philosophical views, Abduh was a Sufi, a Pantheist and a Universalist. He thought much about the possibility of reforming religious dogma, and could agree to any surah from the Koran given by the Prophet Muhammad, but was also able to argue with some of the clerics' guidelines governing the law of Muslims on earth.

Ever since I met Abduh for the first time, he has been close to me as a brother. In recent months he has spent much time in the Middle and Near East countries preaching the New Faith among Muslims. And the results of his tireless work, his faith in what he is doing, can be witnessed here and now!

It is well known how Muslims in their majority are intolerant of any innovations, especially of the idea of uniting with Jews, Christians, and other non-Muslims. It was, and still is, blasphemy for them, which made many afraid not only to follow but even to listen to Abduh's speeches.

Now you can see for yourself how many Muslims have come over to our side! And this is an undeniable and amazing victory for Tahir Abduh! This is our common victory! We bow our heads to his ashes and his holy soul!

Oh, my brothers and sisters, we bury this man according to the laws and customs of his fathers and grandfathers. We are not Kafirs and we are not against the Quran and the Prophet Muhammad, we are not against the Shariah. But we urge you, Muslims, to stop seeing enemies in people of other faiths, but to see them as people like you, who believe in the Creator, our One Almighty! We preach the same among Christians, Jews, Hindus, and Buddhists.

Mankind-haters, aggressive people who do not respect God will never be able to stop us, because our Faith is strong, the Lord expects us to respect one another, not only because we are all human, but because we have the same Protector!

What we all have in common is:

1) a common God,

2) and a common home - planet Earth.

People who come to this simple truth will learn to respect each other and will never take up weapons again!

The Quran tells of continuity from the Torah, and in the Old Testament, we can learn that Abraham's children, Ishmael and Isaac, are blood brothers. This means that Moses and Mohammed both heard the voice of the same God, the One Almighty.

God first chose the Jewish people, who believed in him as the One and Undivided One. Then through the Buddha, He turned the Far-Eastern world to Faith. Later, when the time was right, through Christ the Faith spread to Europe and parts of Asia. And finally, through Mohammed, it found its followers in the East. And the nations of the world gave their names to the One Almighty, because they spoke different languages.

Once again, I am in no way rejecting anything holy or wise that has been suffered by the various religions over the thousands of years. But I ask you, people, to think about what the great son of the Arab people, Abduh Tahir, sacrificed his life for! He did it for the sake of our rapprochement, trying to achieve mutual understanding between the nations, wishing to teach us to see all the good, kind and wise things that religions, traditions and customs of all humanity bear in themselves!

So, for example, we should learn the wisdom of life that the Buddhists and Taoists have accumulated. The prophets Buddha and Lao Tzu taught patience, calmness, and optimism. These qualities will help fight such diabolical traits of the human character as aggressiveness, hatred, intolerance, pessimism, envy and anger.

If someone tells you that the more infidels you destroy on earth, the more pleasures you will experience in Paradise, don't believe them! It is a vile lie! Today's "infidels" are not the pagans the Quran speaks of. They believe in the same God you worship. Jews and Christians cannot be "infidels" to Muslims, and vice versa. They all believe in the same Creator and therefore are faithful!

Our glorious prophets from Abraham to Mohammed were not kings or emperors, nor did they have countless riches. But they possessed the souls of millions of people, and for thousands of years, mankind has believed their words! They never taught us to kill our spiritual brothers. On the contrary, through our prophets, the Almighty has gradually guided and continues to guide us to a Single Faith in Him. Faith in the Creator ignites the divine spark in the human soul, and the fear of the Almighty drives humanity to live according to God's commandments, which proclaim love for others and obedience to the law. The Almighty gave mankind a common morality. Through his messengers, God demanded that people behave with decency and dignity toward one another.

My brothers, do not expect to be rewarded by the Almighty by destroying people of other religions, for they are his children, just as you are! The Almighty will not forgive you for fratricide!

Our Faith is the Faith in One God, only through it can we come to One Humanity. How, you may ask? Only by bringing peace and respect to others! There is no other way, everything else is from the evil.

The point of our mission is that every person and every nation learns to appreciate the dignity and differences in another person and nation. This is what the Creator wants from us, the people of the world!

Our Faith is the Faith of Creation and Respect!

Perhaps respect is a less powerful feeling than love, but beyond love is kindness, beyond kindness is respect, but beyond respect are hatred and evil. That line must not be crossed! This is the minimum I ask of the people of the world!

May the Almighty help us all!

Chapter 21

When Joseph returned to New York after Abduh's funeral, it took a long time for him to accept the loss of a devoted brother-in-arms.

David informed him that powerful new friends, representatives of big business, insistently seek a meeting with him.

- You know, this is God's providence, because time is not waiting; we need to act. Missionary work alone will not complete our mission on earth. Your powerful friends can help us, since my immediate goal is to bring to a common denominator the contradictions which lie between Azerbaijan and Armenia, and thus to settle the long-standing discord. By their example, we will show the world that our Faith is valid and strong.

- Why did you choose the Karabakh conflict? - David asked with surprise and after a pause continued: - And how can our powerful tycoons help in this case?

- They can arrange official meetings with the leaders of these states for me. And then we will see, Joseph answered the second question of his friend, deliberately ignoring the first.

Joseph and David were brought to a downtown Manhattan business center near famous Wall Street. They entered a dark glass skyscraper with a person already waiting for them in the lobby. The high-speed elevator soared noiselessly upward. In a minute they were met at the office entrance by a lively gray-haired man who introduced himself as Mr. Higgins. The guests entered the air-conditioned room and sat in armchairs around a small table with soft drinks on it.

Mr. Higgins explained that he represents a major American business and was empowered to speak on behalf of his management. David was then solemnly presented with a business card.

His lean, elongated face, sunken cheeks, and elongated chin made him look like an old-school prim English aristocrat. His slightly curly gray hair was combed back and accentuated the height of his forehead. He was dressed in an immaculate navy suit; a bright red bowtie, which replaced a tie, stood out sharply against the snow-white shirt and added charm to his appearance.

- We are monitoring your activities closely. And I have to admire you - it's impressive! You truly look like a prophet of the twenty-first century.

- Mr. Higgins, I thank you for such a flattering assessment of my activity, but let me ask you, who do you mean by the pronoun "we"?

- We are the heads of multinational corporations, he answered bluntly.

Joseph paused, and Mr. Higgins continued:

- I assure you, these are the most powerful organizations, on which the whole modern world economy is based.

- Why did my humble person so interested these all-powerful people?

- I won't waste your time with long explanations. Note only that it always seemed to people - or rather, they wanted to believe it - that the world is ruled not by official heads of states, but by the Zion sages, or by the Great Masonic Lodge, or some other powerful secret sect. Without going into details, I will directly say that the modern economy is ruled by transnational corporations.

Mr. Higgins interrupted his speech to take a sip of coffee. Joseph continued to remain silent.

- The leaders of these organizations are interested in your religious activities because it fits their long-term strategy. Forgive me for being so rudely frank.

- I've always preferred harsh truths to sweet lies.

- That's fine! Your idea of one world religion for all mankind is very appealing, even if it looks utopian nowadays. But we are interested in it because it contributes to the process of globalization, which is our priority. On the one hand, we can say that globalization is the origin of transnational corporations, and on the other hand, transnational corporations themselves came into being through integration. In general, everything here is interdependent. I apologize for my rambling explanation.

- I understand, Mr. Higgins. But how can I help you?

- Let's cooperate. Work together. And perhaps our business will be more successful.

- But belief in God is not business or commerce. It is a sacred action for every person. The way to believe in God is through the soul, not through cold reasoning and sober calculation.

- Yes, I absolutely agree with you. They are completely different spheres of activity. But if our goals are the same, why not unite?

- And how do you see it?

- You'll get financial help from us. By the way, how do you like your new headquarters? - Mr. Higgins turned his head toward David.

- I would like to take this opportunity, sir, to thank you very much. I already talked to Michael and I thanked him. It's a beautiful office! - He replied, broadly smiling.

Mr. Higgins turned to Joseph again:

- Next, we could establish a fund in your name or the name of your religious organization. It would subsidize your activities as needed. What do you think?

- Any selfless help in bringing people to the Faith in the One Creator would be welcomed by me, for it is a God-pleasing cause.

On reflection, Joseph added:

- Globalization is good because, despite the unfair economic structure of the world, it is possible to solve important world problems together, such as poverty, poor health care, and ethnic conflicts.

- Yes, it is. But unfortunately, globalism is met with strong resistance from social and political movements that try to blame transnational corporations for all the negativity that has accumulated over the years. They believe that almost the entire world economy and its rapaciously used resources belong to a bunch of people who don't give a damn about the rest of humanity.

I will tell you frankly, despite the fact that transnational corporations are the de facto masters of the world, confrontation with the anti-globalists is growing. Discontent in Muslim countries is growing rapidly.

I understand that it is very premature and even utopian to speak of a one-world government, but a one-world religion is negotiable. Belief in One God is as necessary to us as Christianity was to ancient Rome. Transnational corporations can exist without economic borders, they are not interested in nationalities and traditions, they are only interested in money and resources, i.e. in inter-state matters.

The only possibility of economic integration, in which transnational corporations would make their fabulous profits, is the presence of government, in other words, power. This, in turn, further divides an already divided world. The result is a vicious circle from which we must find a way out. Your religious activities will help us to break it.

- You may be right, but we should also understand ordinary citizens who can draw parallels between the unbelievable profits of your corporations and the poverty of entire nations. However, this is not the place for discussion. On the contrary, I appreciate your commitment to our movement, and I am grateful for your support for the unification of humanity based on Faith in One Creator. I am well aware that the modern world order adheres to the concept and practice of the unlimited sovereignty of nations. This, in turn, means that each country has the right to pursue its goals by military means. In such an arrangement, every nation must be prepared for such an outcome, and thus must try its best to outdo any other. This desire has subordinated, is subordinating, and will continue to subordinate the entire social life of humanity and poison the younger generations long before the catastrophe itself falls on their heads. We must not tolerate it, for the time has come when Faith in the One Creator will unite us in a single spiritual space.

As for our agreement, Mr. Higgins, you must clearly understand that I will not fall for any tricks or intrigues, for I am here on this earth on an important mission. This is God's work, and I must finish it with clean hands.

Mr. Higgins listened to Joseph with a deferential expression, not giving away his disbelief for a moment. But this wise and experienced man could sense all the power coming from Joseph. His words were so compelling that one wanted to follow him and do what he said.

After Joseph and David left the office, Mr. Higgins was quite impressed for some time.

Chapter 22

The next day David called Michael and told him of Joseph's request to arrange a meeting with the presidents of Armenia and Azerbaijan. He was not surprised at all,

Michael promised to call back in three days.

Exactly at the appointed time he contacted David and informed him that basically, he had received a positive answer. The only thing required was to make a plan of a diplomatic tour of Transcaucasia, specifying the route and exact dates of visit - in short, the whole protocol part of Joseph's visits.

The first meeting was to be with the head of Armenia.

Joseph flew to Yerevan the very next day. In the morning he was brought to the residence of the head of state. The president was waiting for the famous guest in his office, where Joseph was escorted from the reception. The head stepped out from behind a large desk and headed towards Joseph. As they shook hands, their eyes studied each other intently.

The Armenian President was a tall, thin man with a pleasant smile on his face. He pointed the guest to a large chair and sat opposite. An assistant sat next to him.

- My consultant will be with us, if you don't mind, he explained.

Joseph nodded his head in agreement.

- Rumor has it that you are originally from... - the President paused.

- ...from Baku, Joseph continued his thought. - It's true, I was born in that city.

- Unbelievable! I myself am from Karabakh, but I lived and worked in the capital of Azerbaijan.

- Maybe this helps us to understand each other better. I know that negotiations between Armenia and Azerbaijan have been going on for many years, but without results. Mr. President, have you heard about the Faith that my followers and I preach around the world?

- Of course! Your teachings are extremely attractive, but unrealistic, pardon my frankness. Humanity is not yet ready for it.

- Yes, you are right, humanity is not mature enough. But tell me, were people ready for the sermons of Christ or Moses or Mohammed? Or perhaps the words of Buddha and Krishna? I can assure you, that even less than modern people are for the New Faith. So it is never too early to start something, especially for the good of people. Gradually humanity will follow this Faith, will accept it. What I intend to offer you is based precisely on the idea of the One Creator, which does not divide the Armenian and the Azerbaijani. Yes, they have different traditions, but the Almighty is one, and this is the most important thing. Believing in this will help find common ground between the two nations.

Joseph had already managed to become a skilled orator, who could win over anyone. Perfectly simple words, trivial or sometimes sounding on the verge of fiction, acquired deep meaning in his mouth, and people listened to him, as if imbued with faith in these proclamations.

The same thing was now happening to the president. An experienced, intelligent, cunning and shrewd politician, he suddenly felt weak and hesitant, felt a special, alluring magnetism reaching deep into his heart. In fear, the head of state suddenly imagined what might await him if he accepted the proposal of such an extraordinary man. He realized that he would not last a month in office if he decided to carry out Joseph's plan.

Joseph, meanwhile, talked about the coexistence of Armenians and Azerbaijanis on the basis of an economic contract. He planned to create a free economic zone in the territory of Nagorno-Karabakh and preferably in the border territories of Azerbaijan, currently uninhabitable due to its ruined infrastructure. Its management was to be entrusted to a special directorate, which could include representatives of transnational investor companies and top managers from Azerbaijan and Armenia. Any political superstructure was ruled out; only economic structures like a giant syndicate should operate in the zone. International corporations responsible for developing Nagorno-Karabakh's economy agreed to sponsor the experiment. International peacekeeping troops would be responsible for the security of the territory. The free economic zone will be open for free travel both to Azerbaijan and Armenia. It will be enough to show the passport of a citizen of one of these countries. A visa regime is planned for other visitors. All refugees will be allowed to return to their abandoned homes without hindrance. If so desired by residents of Armenia or Azerbaijan, a committee under the Board of Directors will consider each application individually.

It may take twenty or thirty years to implement this project - that's for specialists to decide. During this time, Armenians and Azerbaijanis will learn to live and work together again, their everyday lives will improve, and economic growth will begin. And only then, in completely different psychological, moral and economic conditions, as well as with the guaranteed security of all people living on this land, Azerbaijan and Armenia will be able to make a decision on the political status of Nagorno-Karabakh.

Always very cautious, the Armenian president said he liked Joseph's plan but needed a few days to think about it.

The same evening Joseph flew to Baku.

The Azerbaijani authorities knew that the famous guest was their compatriot, so they met him at the airport with all the pompousness appropriate to the Caucasus. He was welcomed by the head of the presidential administration, several members of the Mejlis and officials holding high positions in the state.

He was scheduled to have a meeting with the Azerbaijani president the next morning. Joseph was taken to a luxurious palace where the most high-ranking guests were accommodated. The mansion was located in the center of the city, more precisely at the bottom of Nagorny Park, near the boulevard where Joseph was strolling with Azad. Joseph was reminded of the endless rows of soldiers' graves, among which was Rafik's grave.

The guest was escorted to the apartment and left alone. Without noticing the luxury around him, Joseph took a shower and went straight to bed. Long flights always tired him out.

The car came to pick him up at eleven o'clock in the morning. Joseph was driven to the president's residence, where five or six people were already waiting for him in the large reception room, and Joseph walked past them into the beautifully furnished office.

He immediately saw the head of state rushing toward him with welcoming words:

- Good to see you, distinguished Joseph, in your homeland! Please make yourself at home!

He shook his guest's hand firmly, then took him under his elbow and rather familiarly, as if they were old pals, led him toward the armchairs by which there were juices and fruit on a long, low table.

- Please, sit down and help yourselves.

- Thank you for the warm welcome! - answered Joseph, a little surprised by the informal mood.

- What Baku school did you graduate from? - the president suddenly asked.

- I went to school number eight.

- And I studied in the sixth! - the head of the country said jovially and continued: - You have a familiar face. It seems to me that when we were young, we could have easily met. Although so much time has passed...

- It is quite possible, because in Baku many people knew each other, especially those who lived and studied in the center of the city.

- Yes, yes, that's right! - There was a hint of nostalgia in the president's voice.

There was silence for a while. Everyone was deep in thought for a while.

- No matter what they say, we had a good childhood and youth, he sighed sadly. It was obvious that his thoughts were somewhere far away.

- Yes, the Baku people were famous throughout the Soviet Union. It was a special quasi-nationality, Joseph added.

- And everyone was friendly and lived soul to soul... Could we have even imagined at that time how much we would experience?

- The spirit that reigned in Baku in those years was really real. And the most phenomenal is that it existed despite the historical background, despite the political and economic situation, despite everything! Perhaps it was something divine. We can say with confidence that God, by the example of Baku, showed people a true commonwealth of nations, based on spiritual closeness. God was with us at the time, but people did not notice His gift. The time of political cataclysms came and the child was thrown out of the trough with the water. Now another miracle happened, and God condescended to His servant Joseph and entrusted me with the great mission of sowing peace and respect among nations.

- I think we should start with individuals and then work with nations, the president suggested.

- You know, at the time of Jesus Christ and Mohammed, not to mention Moses and Buddha, nations lived in isolation, sometimes unaware of each other's existence. They rarely faced each other, they were territorially separated. The world is very different now. It has shrunk so much that it is possible to fly around the entire earth in twenty-four hours in an airplane. Economic, political and military integration has reached such proportions that it has become simply dangerous to live on our planet without peace and mutual respect.

- Yes, of course, you're right, the head said respectfully.

- I think you'll understand my natural, purely human desire to re-establish peace in the land of Azerbaijan, where I lost people close to me.

- And Joseph told about his friends killed in Karabakh and Chechnya.

- I sympathize with your grief and offer my condolences to all those whose loved ones gave their lives for our land.

- The dead cannot be brought back. Now we must think about the living. Both Armenians and Azerbaijanis believe in the same Creator God. There is no antagonism between them, as between all the peoples of the world, even if they don't realize it now. In fact, they are bound together by an invisible spiritual thread, based on faith in the One Almighty. All religious barriers between nations are the work of humans, not of God.

- I am familiar with your views, but you should understand that our conflict is far from being a religious one, since few people here care that Armenians are Christians and Azerbaijanis are Muslims. You, more than anyone else, should know that our nations are not so religious as to manipulate this. And the fact that some officials interpret this conflict in terms of a clash of civilizations and religions is pure profanation, a propagandistic lie, leading to an even greater confrontation between our nations. So to speak, a beautiful, spectacular glossy cover, under which dirty political deeds are committed.

- Yes, I know it is. But I believe in my purpose. My Faith can convince people to change their views.

- We would be only glad to do so. But Karabakh is our land, and we will never agree, even for the sake of world peace, to give it to Armenians.

- But you must agree, Mr. President, that in order to give something away or not, you must at least have it. You've been trying to do that for more than ten years.

- If we have to, we'll try for another twenty, just to get what we want! - Suddenly his interlocutor interrupted him abruptly.

- Excuse me, but I am not here to start a polemic with you.

- I am elected to defend the interests of the Azerbaijani people! The people and I, as the leader of the nation, do not intend to give Armenians even an inch of our territory!

- And I am not asking you to do that.

And Joseph introduced to the head his plan to resolve the conflict by temporarily turning the disputed area into a free economic zone where Azerbaijanis and Armenians will work together and where transnational companies will invest. God willing, the economic prosperity of the region and time will do its work - ordinary people will forgive all the misfortune and evil they have caused each other.

- And who will be in charge of this territory, to whom will it belong? - With a faint smile on his lips, the President asked.

- The territory of Karabakh has belonged to Azerbaijan, and will continue to belong to Azerbaijan. Azerbaijan is supposed to pass this zone for long term rent. The terms will be coordinated with the economical sponsors who will calculate how long it will take to raise the region on its feet. Any political superstructure will be eliminated. Only economic management organizations, such as the Board of Directors, will be created, which will include Azerbaijani and Armenian specialists, as well as foreign creditors. They will become the real managers of the zone for the duration of the contract. There will be no Azerbaijani, Armenian, or Karabakh military there. International peacekeeping forces of the European Union will control the region. The police will be recruited from the local population. A special commission will start working under the board of directors to control the observance of human rights in the region, and it will consist of the most respected people - aksakals, who are respected and listened to by the local population. Everyone who has lived on this land before will be able to return home.

After a short pause the President said:

- In any case, the Azerbaijani people have the last word. We will address to it and find out its opinion. I will also think about it and give you my answer.

- Mr. President, let me make an urgent request of you! I would like to speak to people in Baku and other regions of the country.

- Why do you need my permission, dear Joseph? We have a free country, and everyone can meet with anyone and anywhere, within the limits of the existing law.

- Then I'll change my message a little. Would you be so kind as to facilitate my meetings with the public? After all, it is impossible to organize public events without the cooperation of the local authorities.

- Oh yes, of course! Everything will be all right. You don't have to worry about that.

- One more thing, Mr. President. I was born in Baku and I lost my friends here. Believe me, I came back here to help the Azerbaijani people in this difficult time. I wish my deceased friend's daughter living in Armenia could see her poor grandmother living in Baku.

The next day Joseph flew to Khankendi1 , the district center of Nagorno-Karabakh.

(In Soviet times, the capital of the Nagorno-Karabakh Autonomous Region was called Stepanakert. After the armed conflict, Baku renamed, or rather, returned the pre-revolutionary name - Khankendi. But Armenians continue to call the city, as in Soviet times, Stepanakert).

David organized meetings of Joseph's closest associates with the deputy foreign ministers of Russia, France, and representatives of the United States Department of State. All of these countries involved in the negotiation process to resolve the Karabakh conflict welcomed Joseph's peace initiative. Everyone was greatly influenced by the special aura that accompanied him. People really began to believe and hope that this man would be able to do the nearly impossible: to resolve a longstanding, complicated inter-ethnic issue in a way that was fair to both sides.

In Stepanakert, Joseph was warmly welcomed by the local authorities led by the President and Speaker of the Karabakh Parliament. The guests were put in cars and driven to a new hotel in the city center.

In the evening, the entire delegation was invited to a gala dinner at a restaurant where the entire Karabakh leadership was gathered. The table was lavish in the Caucasian way, and plenty of drinks were served. The Karabakh people did their best for the American guests, as they were flattered by the attention of such a world-famous man as Joseph.

But he, who was considered the Messiah, the last prophet, and almost a messenger of God, sat modestly, ate little, and only occasionally sipped on a glass of thick, tart red wine made from local grape varieties. At the end of the meal, he asked for a word, and everyone fell silent.

- My dear brothers and sisters! Thank you for the bread and salt, and thank you for the warm, friendly welcome! I have come here with the goal of bringing peace back to this beautiful and long-suffering land. My dream is that we all wake up and look with different eyes around us, at the people around us. Believe me, there is nothing like neighborly mutual respect and peaceful existence! This land is very precious to me. I was born near you and lost my friends here.

I want to try with you to turn this land into a place of peace, where people can work, create families, and raise children!

The next day Joseph met with the Karabakh leadership and explained the essence of his project. There was skepticism and uncertainty on the faces of those in power, but they did not show direct displeasure and behaved respectfully.

At the end of his talk, Joseph asked permission to address the people in the main square of the city.

In the middle of the same day, the people began to assemble to hear the distinguished guest. People even came from distant villages to hear him.

Joseph stood on the platform. His thin elongated face, his long hair flapping in the wind, and his small beard made him look like the prophets of old.

- Brothers and sisters! - as always, he began his speech. - The Almighty once again gives us a chance to gather our spirits and shake off the devil's sleepiness and blindness! He again calls his children to open their eyes and wake up from the bad dream in which we all still dwell!

What will this awakening and purification do for us? We will see and realize our Creator of the universe and the earth in a new way! We will realize that he is One and Undivided. God is everything, He is present in every person, belongs to all of us, and we all belong to Him. When we believe this, we will look at each other with different eyes.

Nations will realize that they belong to the One God, that all religions call people to worship the One Almighty. He may be called by different names, but He is One. This realization of Oneness and Indivisibility will help us reduce the suffering we feel because of endless strife, because of the devil's sense of mutual hostility, mistrust and alienation. Faith in One God will be the bridge that will unite Azerbaijanis and Armenians, help overcome the superficial sense of hostility and help people forgive each other. For the sake of the future, for the sake of our children, both sides must learn to live in peace and harmony! For there is no other way!

Unpleasant shouts were heard from the crowd. The chorus of dissatisfied voices began to grow, which prevented Joseph from speaking. One of the organizers of the performance waved his hands frantically, trying to calm the crowd. But the crowd did not calm down and became more and more heated.

Finally, an elderly man with gray hair and a completely white beard came out of the front row, approached Joseph and said:

- You speak in the name of God, but we do not know who you are.

- Send him away, he is a spy from Azerbaijan! - someone shouted angrily.

The elder shouted angrily into the crowd:

- People, I ask only one thing of you: please do not insult!

And he continued:

- Here you say that we should live and work together with the Azerbaijanis. But did you know that every third person here has lost a son, father or brother defending their land from them? The Azerbaijanis are our enemies, and we can no longer live with them. And our children and our grandchildren will never forget it!

The old man fell silent. And the crowd erupted in cheers, applauding his words. Then there were some shouts of encouragement to disperse, so as not to waste time and listen to the rascals.

The crowd quickly dwindled, and Joseph and his three assistants watched the scene motionlessly.

Soon all that was left of the great crowd was a small group that stood hesitantly in place, looking at the preacher.

Joseph stepped toward them. When he saw this, the eldest among them stepped toward him.

- Excuse our compatriots... Our people are harsh and rude. But you should also understand them. We've been through so much here...

- I'm not offended at all. They will understand that they are wrong. It just really takes time.

In front of Joseph stood a middle-aged, intelligent-looking man in a suit without a tie. He resembled a country teacher.

- Honorable Joseph, you have no idea what an honor it is for us to see you in Stepanakert. I am so happy that I have the opportunity to meet you in person! My name is Ruben, I work at a school here, I teach physics and at the same time I am the head of the educational department. You are really doing a God-pleasing job, trying to reconcile us with the Azerbaijanis. My comrades and I, he pointed to the people standing to the side, are in complete solidarity with you. But we are in minority here, and nobody listens to us. We are almost seen as traitors.

- It doesn't matter that there are only a few of you, what matters is that you exist. Dear Ruben, you and your friends are on the right path! If you are strong in your belief that the only way to ensure a normal and decent life for the children of this land is peaceful coexistence with your neighbors on a fair basis, this belief will surely be transmitted to others!

Since Joseph and his companions were scheduled to leave the next day, Ruben invited them to his house for dinner.

At home, he introduced the Americans to his family - his wife, Vera, and his daughter, Svetlana, who had come from Yerevan to stay with her parents for a few days. Joseph was attracted to the young, beautiful, and intelligent girl. They talked a lot about God and people, about the future, and hope for the best.

- I monitor your religious activities via the internet and am very sympathetic to your ideas. Oh, now I feel like I'm dreaming! You, such a world-famous man - and suddenly you're sitting in my father's house talking to a simple girl!

- People are not divided into simple and not simple. We all have the spark of God, because human beings came into being according to God's will, and each of us has a part of God's Spirit in us, which we call the soul. Even though the Bible says that woman came from the rib of

Adam, I stand for the equal rights of man and woman. And I dare say that the power of the divine spark in women is not less than it is in men. But let's talk about you. What do you do?

- I teach literature and the Russian language at Yerevan State Pedagogical Institute. After graduation, I was left as an assistant at the department, and since last year I started lecturing, - says Svetlana proudly.

- Oh, how interesting. I used to love reading books. But lately, I haven't had time, - Joseph confessed.

- Did you really communicate with God? - she suddenly asked.

- No, I didn't. The great prophets came to me in a dream, and I talked to them. They instructed me in the name of God and convinced me that I would be able to fulfill the mission entrusted to me by the Almighty. You may ask, why me? I have no answer. This is God's providence.

- Joseph, I understand the idea you bring to people. But they tell and write so many horror stories about Azerbaijanis that it's hard for an average person to imagine how he or she can get along with such people.

- I was born and lived in Azerbaijan. Believe me, they are the same people as Armenians. I believe that people gradually learn to listen to their hearts. To move towards God one needs work of the soul, and on this way, one can understand that we are all human beings and we all deserve a good and peaceful life. Our dream is that Azerbaijani and Armenian children will never take up weapons again and, with the help of adults, learn to live and work together.

- Yes, I agree. This mutual hatred must stop. The constant enmity turns our life into hell, Svetlana sighed heavily.

In parting, Ruben gave Joseph a little advice: if the preacher really wants to help the two nations, he should move to Karabakh for a while for the memory of his fallen friends, for the sake of the Faith, because it is impossible to solve this difficult problem with only proclamations.

Chapter 23

Sitting in the "Boeing" that was taking him to New York, Joseph was well aware that watching the events in Karabakh from the outside would actually bring him nothing.

He was well aware of the heavy burden he had voluntarily placed on his shoulders. But his faith in his divine mission gave him the strength to hope that he would see it through.

Soon after his arrival, he received bad news from Karabakh: Ruben had been severely beaten by unknown assailants and was in the hospital. Joseph was very upset. Ruben's last words echoed in his memory: You have to be here. Without your presence, the case would not progress.

And it really wasn't making any progress. Everyone around him was only feeding Joseph promises of their assistance, but no one was doing anything. Armenia did not want to take troops out of Karabakh, the European Union was in no hurry to approve Joseph's plan. Azerbaijan was silent, never responding to his proposal. Everyone was asking for a postponement, but in fact, they were stalling for time. This is the reason why such conflicts become chronic and simmer for decades. The winner or the stronger party is interested in prolonging the dispute, because they already dominate the disputed territory. The loser or weaker party, on the other hand, wants to restore the situation that existed before the conflict began. They have already lost everything, so they are in no hurry to document the real state of affairs.

Joseph decided to fly urgently to Karabakh. Upon learning of this, David tried to dissuade him from this dangerous venture:

- Joseph, what are you doing? We have so many urgent things to do! We can't do it without you.

- David, my place is over there. And here you can handle it alone. You must understand, I have to do it! Otherwise, it makes no sense.

- Oh, modern prophets, how impatient you are! Think of Christ, and how long it took him to explain his teachings to the people and not demand instant change. That process took hundreds of years! You are only commissioned to put the seed into fertile ground, and then it will survive, break through, grow, and blossom by itself.

- Yes, but Christ performed miracles that confirmed his divine nature. The resolution of the Karabakh conflict today is also a kind of miracle, after which people will no longer doubt us.

Two days after Joseph's departure from Karabakh, Ruben and his like-minded associates organized a demonstration that brought together the few followers of the New Faith as well as representatives of various parties. The party that Ruben led was called the Party of Reconciliation.

The teacher addressed the crowd with an encouraging speech:

- I'll be brief. There is a real opportunity to resolve our long-standing conflict with the Azerbaijanis. God is with us, and we must help the Venerable Joseph in his holy mission. Understand, people, my companions and I are thinking first of all about our children and grandchildren, who will have to live in this land next to the Azerbaijanis! So are we going to leave them such a terrible legacy - ceaseless wars? Why condemn them to constant fear, to put them at risk, instead of making peace in this land, or at least moving in that direction?

This is important to begin without delay! The conflict has been going on for over a decade. Our children, who were teenagers then, unlike us, have no Azerbaijani friends. Yes, we, their fathers and grandfathers, have been feuding with each other all this time, although most of our generation has a peaceful past when we were friends with our neighbors. These personal ties are very important in solving the problem, because it is one thing to try to reconcile a certain Ashot, who knew a certain Mammad, and quite another to try to reconcile an abstract Armenian and an Azerbaijani. After all, it will be much more difficult to resolve these ongoing quarrels after our children come to take our place than it is now!

Shouts of approval could be heard from the crowd. Some began to recall their friends or Azerbaijani neighbors, some amusing episodes or good stories from the past that made them smile.

- And we will achieve peace, Ruben continued, with compromises, mutual concessions, and a sense of responsibility to posterity, but not through the pursuit of vested political and economic interests.

This time the speaker was greeted with threatening shouts. An old friend from the radical Dashnaktsu-Tun party approached him:

- Listen, Ruben, as a friend I'm asking you to stop talking like this...

- Are you threatening me?

- No, I'm asking you as an old friend, don't provoke people, it's very serious. You've gone too far!

Despite the threats, Ruben went on to talk about the Reconciliation Party initiative: an opportunity to meet with an Azerbaijani organization close in spirit to their party, which also seeks peace and mutual compromise for a peaceful future for their children and grandchildren. The meeting was to be held in neutral territory in Tbilisi. This news infuriated the Dashnaks, and they decided to teach Ruben a lesson.

The teacher had worked late that day and arrived home after dark. As usual, when he opened the gate, he went into his garden and at that moment he felt severe pain in the back of his head, after which he lost consciousness.

...Through the heavy unconsciousness, he could hear someone's bitter sobs. Ruben tried to open his eyes, but a sharp pain pierced his throat and he switched off again.

After a while he regained consciousness. He cautiously opened his eyes and at the same time, he remembered everything...

There's the gate, he walks into his front yard... There he was being hit on the head with something heavy... And now he was lying in a hospital bed with his wife sitting beside him, wailing and sobbing intermittently.

Seeing her husband awake, Vera involuntarily cried out. She ran to call a nurse or a doctor.

- I told you, stay out of this politics! Do you want to leave behind three orphans and a widow? If you don't think of yourself, at least think of the children and me! - She cried and yelled.

The doctors diagnosed the patient with two broken ribs and a severe concussion. The doctor assured him that Ruben was lucky, otherwise, such a blow could have been fatal.

An investigator came and wrote down the victim's testimony. There were no witnesses to the accident. The neighbors did not see or hear anything.

Chapter 24

Joseph and his two assistants arrived in Yerevan and immediately boarded a small plane that made strange noises. Throughout the flight, the machine wobbled from time to time, shaking its passengers.

Joseph was carrying cargo to Stepanakert. They were brand new computers for the school where Ruben worked. This time his welcome was less pompous. The head of the city and the director of the school were present. The guests were taken to a hotel, and the shipment was sent to the school.

After a while, a car came to pick Joseph up. It was a Soviet-era model six Zhiguli. Joseph went to Ruben's house to visit his wife, since it was too late to go to the hospital. There he saw Svetlana, who had flown to Stepanakert as soon as she heard about her father's accident. All this time the image of Ruben's daughter stood before Joseph.

That evening they stayed up late. Joseph comforted the women as much as he could.

- Please, Joseph, tell my father not to be involved in politics anymore! You see how dangerous it is. He will listen to you, Svetlana asked, almost crying.

- Your father is doing a God-pleasing job and you can be rightly proud of him. Yes, it involves a risk to life, but such people who fight for peace and mutual respect become national heroes, unlike those who call for hatred and murder.

At night, lying in his hotel bed, Joseph could not sleep for a long time. He kept thinking about Sveta. He liked her more and more. With her, he felt an inner peace. His heart clenched sweetly when her beautiful eyes looked at him excitedly.

The next day, right from the morning, Joseph went to the hospital. Ruben was already half lying in his bed. There were four other people in the room with him. The assistants stayed in the corridor, and Joseph went inside, greeted everyone, and sat down next to his friend.

- How are you feeling, my friend?

- I'm recovering.

- Your wife is very worried, but I calmed her down as much as I could.

- Thank you, Joseph, for everything. I'm so glad you came. We'll get a lot done together.

- Listen, Ruben, I brought computers for the kids...

- I don't know how to thank you. You're a magician, you can do anything. The kids will be happy, they needed computers so badly! Wow, you brought it for the whole school! That's great!

- Yes, it is a good deed for our children, - one of the patients nodded his head respectfully.

- The kids will be very happy! - Another one exclaimed.

- When will some adults realize that they should live in a happy and peaceful future? - Ruben asked sadly.

Joseph stayed with him for a while longer and started to say goodbye:

- Ruben, I have come here for a long time. You're right, I should be with you. So get well soon! You know how much important work we have ahead of us. God bless you.

- Yes, Joseph, you never cease to amaze me. Thank you for everything. I'll do my best. But I ask you only one thing: be careful, this is not America here.

On the same day, Joseph presented the new computers in the assembly hall of the school, which was filled to capacity with children, teachers, and parents.

The principal of the school spoke first. He thanked the generous patron on behalf of the teachers and parents for such a rich and necessary gift for the students. Then the word was given to Joseph:

- My dear children, dear parents and teachers! Our younger generation deserves everything they need for a decent life. People like Ruben and I, with God's help, strive to make this the norm. To do this, you, adults need to work toward a peaceful life, only then God's help can come to you. We urge you to bury the hatchet and direct all your efforts toward creating a common future together with your neighboring Azerbaijanis!

The audience froze and listened quietly to Joseph.

- Life is not just a game, life is a divine game. But the rules are the same. It cannot be played with one goal. God created us so that we can never live in isolation. And one of our responsibilities is to learn to live alongside other peoples in peace and harmony, learning to respect our neighbor's traditions on mutually acceptable terms. God wants peace and respect between people and nations! God wants reconciliation...

Joseph's repeated visit to Karabakh, his feverish activity and intention to settle here for an indefinite period alarmed. Military commanders of Russian troops stationed in Karabakh and Armenia. Naturally, they did not see God's purpose or Joseph's divine mission behind all this, but rather the hand of Washington.

One of the Russian told the president bluntly:

- The Americans are indiscriminate in their methods and are trying, by all means, to take over the whole Caucasus. This must not be allowed to happen under any circumstances!

As a result, there was a secret instruction from above to neutralize the emerging threat from the United States.

In Karabakh, meanwhile, the pacifist slogans of peace and quiet, of being able to live and work with the Azerbaijanis, as it had been recently, were heard more and more frequently. For the children, for the future. And all this was happening under the auspices of the One Almighty, the unifier of nations.

Joseph and Svetlana became very good friends. The beautiful and intelligent girl, oddly enough, were single. By Caucasian standards, she was clearly overdue for a personal life, because she was already twenty-six. Her relatives and friends complained that she was highly selective and she didn't like anyone. So you can stay an old maid, they grumbled. Svetlana was a very independent person. She always acted as she saw fit and did not take advice from her parents and relatives, who from time to time tried to match her with one or another gentleman. All candidates for husbands seemed to her uninteresting and superficial.

When Svetlana first saw Joseph at her parents' house, she fell in love with him at first sight, completely and irrevocably, even before he could say a single word. Of course, she did not hope for reciprocity from such a famous man, but she could do nothing about her feelings. At night she wept silently, trying not to wake anyone. Then she left for Yerevan, where she lived and worked. Here Svetlana tried to forget her beloved, but she did not succeed. She collected all the literature about him, she put his portrait up in her room, and became his zealous follower.

When her father's misfortune happened, the girl immediately flew to Stepanakert, where she met Joseph again. It was God's providence. She could no longer hide her feelings and opened her heart to him.

Joseph was quite embarrassed by such an unusual reaction of the young beauty. Yes, she was young, intelligent, attractive, and he definitely liked her. But now, when he was entrusted with such an important mission, he could not think of personal happiness. Mental worries might have been a hindrance to the work. Joseph was very excited by the love confession. Svetlana's feelings were so frank, pure, and naïve that they disarmed him.

Svetlana did not hope for anything. She knew that they were not destined to be together, and she dared not even dream of becoming Joseph's life partner. Therefore, she concentrated all her thoughts on helping Joseph in his important mission and devoting herself completely to the mission of her chosen one. She never suspected that she was capable of such passionate love.

In the evenings, when Joseph was free, Svetlana would visit him at his hotel, and they would talk for hours about God, peace, people, and everything. She felt like a bird soaring high in the sky, unaware of anyone around her, and lived only for these brief rendezvous.

Stepanakert was a small town, and rumors of their relationship spread quickly through the neighborhood. People made up all sorts of things! They accused Svetlana of disgracing the family, of behaving like a corrupt girl, and so on. Her mother warned the girl, persuaded her, begged her, ordered her not to go to Joseph's hotel and to leave for Yerevan at all. But Svetlana, so happy, all radiant, did not hear or see anything, turned her head and, hugging Vera gustily, said:

- Pay no attention to these rumors.

However, the gossip reached even the hospital where Ruben stayed. And when Svetlana came to visit her father, he asked:

- Daughter, what are these people gossiping about you?

- Daddy, you know the local people very well. It costs them nothing to make things up and slander someone.

- Of course, daughter, I don't believe any of that filthy nonsense. They probably want to smear and disgrace me in this way. But tell me frankly, have you fallen in love with Joseph? Your mother told me about it.

Svetlana, blushing thickly, lowered her eyes:

- So what's the big deal?

- This is not Yerevan, and you should behave appropriately, and not disgrace your family!

- And you, too! Daddy, you are an educated and modern man! What's wrong with a girl communicating with a young unmarried man? Especially a man like Joseph. He's a saint, Dad, you hear, a saint! He has communicated with the prophets themselves. He...

- Sveta, my dear daughter, listen to me, your father... He's no match for you! He will never marry you! He just doesn't care about you.

Svetlana ran out of the room in tears.

At that time Joseph, along with Ruben's friends, was traveling all over Karabakh, from village to village, and talking to people. The local nature struck him with its splendor. Only the Almighty could have created these fabulous mountain landscapes.

By the end of the day the group had reached the border of Nagorno-Karabakh and the Plains, where a military post was located. Without a special order from the authorities, entry was forbidden. The border guard explained that a special pass was required. Basically, no further explanation was needed: one could see everything with his own eyes. A terrible panorama opened up to Joseph, as if he were a participant in a fantasy story. As far as the human eye could see, the abandoned villages were disappearing into the horizon. Desolation and abandonment reigned everywhere. It really was a dead zone, like in Tarkovsky's "Stalker". Such landscapes appeared before Joseph and his companions now.

And yet, relatively recently, life was in full swing here. People could not imagine that they would have to flee from these places, leaving their homes.

The "dead zone" was a buffer section of safe land between Nagorno-Karabakh and the present front line. Recaptured by Armenia from Azerbaijan, it comprised fifteen percent of its entire territory, with a population of one million people expelled in 1993.

The bleak picture made the guests sad.

- Yes, it's not a pretty sight... But what could they do? It was necessary to protect Nagorno-Karabakh from the Azerbaijani artillery, said Ruben's friend Sergey.

- The nature is so beautiful here, said Joseph quietly. - We just have to create conditions in which people can work in peace and move from the Middle Ages to the 21st century. They deserve it!

In a short time Joseph had become so attached to Svetlana that he could no longer imagine even one day without her. The girl's passionate and sincere love struck him to the heart. And Joseph, previously so indifferent to the females, trembled before this unknown energy.

He believed that love was a divine gift and he was not ashamed of his reciprocal feelings.

The only thing tearing at his soul was the realization that he would not be able to create a family, have a wife and children, for he must devote himself wholeheartedly to a higher mission. The days he spent with Svetlana were among the happiest of Joseph's life. In her he found a clever and thoughtful interlocutor who understood everything instantly.

Joseph was thinking about all of this again as he lay in his bed late at night. He could not fall asleep for a long time, and only in the morning did he forget in a restful sleep. He dreamt of his parents asking him to come back home. But he silently shook his head as if refusing them. Then his dead friends appeared to him. They hugged each other, laughed, and called him to them. Joseph, smiling, went towards them and opened his arms for an embrace...

He woke up with a headache. He was awakened by the noise of some truck, which tried in vain to start right under the windows. For some time Joseph could not understand where he was. Suddenly his memory flashed through his mind, and he clutched his head in despair as he recalled the events of the previous evening.

...About ten o'clock he began, as usual, to say goodbye to Svetlana. Usually, Joseph's assistant drove her home. However, yesterday the girl behaved strangely. During the good-bye, she came so close to Joseph that he felt her hot breath. She looked directly into his eyes, and Joseph squeezed her hand in his.

Svetlana slowly brought her face close to his and closed her eyes at the same time. Joseph touched her lips and she passionately embraced him and kissed him back. Joseph embraced Svetlana and felt his legs suddenly go limp and become padded. He had not experienced such pleasure in the embrace of a young girl for a long time. Joseph realized that he was losing control of himself and tried to stop, but Svetlana only pressed harder against him.

They involuntarily took a few steps and collapsed on the bed.

...It was the first time for Svetlana. But she was great. Joseph was over the moon. He had forgotten the last time he had been with a woman. It was as if it had happened in a past life. He surrendered to the impulse of love with a passion he had never expected from himself.

A little later, as they lay snuggled together, Svetlana suddenly cried. Joseph was confused, not knowing what to do, but the girl, seeing his embarrassed face, smiled through her tears. She was crying for joy. Calmly, Joseph looked at her fondly and wiped away the moisture on her cheeks.

- Joseph, I love you so much that I don't know how I can continue to live! I can't live without you.

- My darling, I love you too. I love you so much!

Svetlana closed her eyes, and Joseph began to stroke her beautiful hair.

- Imagine for a moment that the world we live in is a union of people who believe in One Creator God, regardless of religious affiliation, despite language, cultural and traditional differences. Only UNITY. We must fill ourselves with the idea of UNITY. GOD is UNITY and PEACE.

Quietly Svetlana lay silently in the arms of her beloved and listened to his voice. She just melted with happiness.

Closer to twelve o'clock at night the phone rang. It was Svetlana's mother. Only then did the lovers finally wake up and return to the real world. The girl quickly dressed, cleaned herself up, and Joseph's assistant took her home.

This is what happened last night. Joseph felt very uncomfortable. He wondered how he would look the girl's parents in the eye since he knew the Caucasian customs which he had so rashly broken.

Every day Joseph traveled to various district centers and talked to people. His interlocutors were primarily interested in material well-being, the elimination of numerous life and economic problems, the availability of jobs, salaries, and so on. And they were ready to live with the Azerbaijanis only on the condition of a peace agreement.

Joseph saw how much easier it was for him to negotiate with ordinary citizens than with politicians and the military. He saw for himself how tired the people were of being in limbo - neither war nor peace- and wanted certainty, longed to live without a military guarding their safety against possible attack by Azerbaijan.

Today was Joseph's last free day. A great demonstration was planned for tomorrow in Stepanakert Square. All those who had agreed with Joseph's project were to gather there to support him, showing the authorities the true desire of the people to resolve the conflict through economic means. The common people wanted to pay their grievances in the name of the children and their peaceful future. They were willing to work with their sleeves rolled up for the prosperity of their families and the nation. Prosperity and time will heal the wounds and help us forget the bad... We must look forward, stop looking back...

After the planned speech, Joseph was to return to the United States for further high-level talks. Then another trip to Azerbaijan was to take place.

Joseph decided to spend today with his beloved. Svetlana devoted herself to him completely and wholeheartedly, and Joseph blamed himself for not keeping his temper, and begged God to forgive his feelings for the girl he had made a woman.

In the afternoon he picked up Svetlana, asking his assistants to stay at the hotel.

The weather was glorious in May, the spring air stupefying his head, lush bright green vegetation blooming all around, and the birds chirping relentlessly.

They drove along a beautiful unpaved road out of town to take a walk in the woods, get some privacy, and bask in the sun's gentle rays.

Once there, the couple fell impatiently onto the emerald grass and embraced gently. The intoxicating scent of greenery worked like a divine wine drink. The two bodies merged into one and froze in a long kiss.

Then, leaning back, they stretched out their arms and legs, completely relaxed, and closed their eyes.

- What prevents people from understanding each other? Was it only the lack of boundaries of conflicting interests? The conflict of ideas and opinions often causes envy, revenge, anger, and hatred. This is inherent in all human beings. It is the same in the relationship between people. The same vices... - reasoned Svetlana.

Joseph opened his eyes and turned to her:

- The basis of Evil on Earth is pride. It is the worst sin, the apotheosis of limitedness, isolation in one's own self. Fortunately, everyone is infected with this to a different degree. This is the basis of Evil on Earth. And the worst kind of pride is the pride of the intellect.

- What can overcome it in a human being? Is there such a power?

Faith in God? - Svetlana asked.

- A person's inner being does not depend on circumstances, but on whether there is a higher divine origin in him. For believers, the greatest mystery of the universe is the presence of the soul in human beings. If you seek to know yourself, through this you come closer to God. This is how liberation from pride happens. Even though we live in a corrupt world, we can overcome the feelings that divide us. The Spirit of God gives us strength, for we are all children of God. We need only live with the awareness of God, and then enlightenment will come to us.

- People are caught up in cruel circumstances, swamped by daily problems that force them to bend. Sickness and suffering destroy their bodies on a minute-by-minute basis. The guides skilfully find the culprits of one nation's inner troubles among its neighbors, pitting them against one another in their own interests. Where will the strength to fight against all this come from?

- The power of Faith in the One Almighty through the comprehension of the Spirit of God in yourself will enable you to overcome these burdens of earthly life. The main weapon against hatred is the state of happiness of comprehending the divine spiritual origin. In spite of everything. This state is the power that drives you to keep God's commandments. When you are unhappy, you have no desire to do good to yourself or others. Do you know the circumstances under which the Jews received the Torah?

- I only know what is written in the Old Testament, answered Svetlana.

- Then I will tell you. The Jews were the last nation to whom God offered to accept and follow the laws of the Torah. And they responded, "Naase venishma," which means "believe and do, and then analyze and understand." This statement should be made by each person as his life principle. The Lord said: "And let these words which I command you today be on your heart." Notice, not "in your heart," but "on your heart." This means that even if your heart is not yet open enough to accept the commandments, you can study them for now and let them be on your heart. One day, when you are ready, the teachings will penetrate you and these ideas will live in your heart.

Joseph fell silent. And Svetlana lay fascinated by the melody of the speech and the depth of her beloved's thought.

The sun's rays gently caressed their faces, piercing through the thick foliage of mighty perennial trees. Joseph opened his eyes and, rising on his elbows, gently stroked Svetlana's light brown curly hair, shimmering in the light.

- Svetlana, I want to tell you...

He paused for a moment, but then continued:

- I'm sorry about yesterday... I shouldn't have done that.

- What are you talking about, Joseph! You can't even imagine how happy I am!

She rose up after him and gently touched her lips to his forehead.

- Sveta, do you understand... Life, our reality, and our love - it's all so complicated...

- Yes, I perfectly understand. You, as a man, like clarity, certainty, and stability. And we, women, often indulge our feelings and emotions. That's true. I don't need anything else! I'm already happy because I love and am loved. You don't have to worry about anything. Don't think about me! You have affairs of great importance, and I am happy that I have touched at least somehow this God-pleasing plan and became your woman. I belong to you - that's the main thing for me. No matter how my life turns out. Although, of course, being with you is the peak of my dreams.

Joseph smiled.

- Oh, my girl... - He pulled her to him and hugged her tightly.

At that moment a strange shadow covered their faces. Someone stood over their heads.

There were three huge men in front of them, all in camouflage uniforms, with black stockings pulled over their heads. The strangers held axes in their hands. It was clear that these people were not local and most likely Russian military.

Without giving the lovers a moment's hesitation, the two men dragged the girl aside and began tearing her clothes off. Svetlana cried out in rage, resisting desperately. The third towered like a mountain over Joseph and grinned evilly.

- What are you doing, come to your senses! - He sprang toward his beloved but was instantly overtaken by the giant standing in front of him.

- Look, boy, I advise you not to interfere with these guys. They'll have their fun, do their thing, and leave. You get the hell out of here before you piss me off.

- Listen, what's your name?

- It doesn't matter

- I'm a guest in your land, my name is Joseph. I come here with God and peace. This girl is with me. Please, for God's sake, leave her alone and do whatever you want with me!

- Are you out of your mind? These guys are straight, they won't be interested in you!

At this point, Svetlana was thrown to the ground. One held her by the arms, while the other, in a rage, continued to expose her body, whispering:

- Quiet, beauty, be quiet... You'll feel good now... Why are you trembling like a chicken before the execution?

And the poor girl kept crying desperately for help, wriggling in the hands of her rapists.

Joseph once again rushed to rescue her but was again knocked to the ground, and then received a powerful blow to the face. Overcoming the intense pain and wiping his eyes, he barely got up. Blood covered his eyes and he was unsteady.

This time he lunged straight at the giant. The strongman threw his axe to the ground and wrapped his arms around Joseph's neck. Then, after choking him a little, he hit him on the head with all his might. Joseph fell down and lost consciousness.

And in an instant there was silence. Svetlana stopped screaming. One of the rapists had possessed her. She lay senseless on the ground, no longer resisting. The other walked up to the strongman and said:

- It's time, finish him off.

He lifted his axe from the ground and smashed Joseph's head with a full swing. The blood splashed on his pants.

The other muttered:

- Couldn't you have been more careful? Come on, let's get out of here.

And they disappeared quietly, just as they had appeared, into the woods...

Chapter 25

Two telephones were ringing simultaneously in the room where Joseph slept.

Finally, his eyelids, heavy with long and deep sleep, fluttered open, and the man opened his eyes. Slowly moving his eyes from one side to the other, he made sure that he was lying in his bedroom, in an apartment in Manhattan.

Joseph put his hand to his head and touched it. It was unharmed,

but it hurt terribly. He got out of bed, looked in the mirror, and saw his pale face covered with a week's worth of stubble.

"So it was only a dream!" - Joseph guessed, realizing the fantasy of what had happened.

Would the last chance for humanity to survive remain nothing more than a sick man's dream?

The phones were ringing off the hook...

www.ingramcontent.com/pod-product-compliance
Lightning Source LLC
Chambersburg PA
CBHW020241130626
46549CB00005B/1994